REAL **SLOW** COOKING

REAL **SLOW** COOKING

KATHRYN HAWKINS

NEW
HOLLAND

First published in 2010 by New Holland Publishers (UK) Ltd
London • Cape Town • Sydney • Auckland

Garfield House
86–88 Edgware Road
London W2 2EA
United Kingdom
www.newhollandpublishers.com

80 McKenzie Street
Cape Town 8001
South Africa

Unit 1, 66 Gibbes Street
Chatwood
NSW 2067
Australia

218 Lake Road
Northcote
Auckland
New Zealand

ISBN 978 1 84773 708 3

Senior editor: Corinne Masciocchi
Designer: Lucy Parissi
Photographer: Sue Atkinson
Home economy and food styling: Kathryn Hawkins
Production: Laurence Poos
Editorial direction: Rosemary Wilkinson

2 4 6 8 10 9 7 5 3 1

Reproduction by Pica Digital PTE Ltd, Singapore
Printed and bound in Malaysia by Times Offset (M) Sdn Bhd

CONTENTS

INTRODUCTION

Say the words 'slow cooker' to most people and they may remember the revolutionary kitchen appliance of the 1970s but most likely their thoughts will be based around soupy, bland stews with no texture. When I was studying home economics in the mid 80s, we thought that slow cookers (along with pressure cookers, contact grills and electric frying pans) were already old-fashioned and were appliances only our mothers would use – back then, the microwave oven was our appliance of choice and the 'fast food' movement was taking off. And yet, here we are some three decades later, the slow cooker is back and is once again fast becoming a contemporary kitchen must-have.

I'll admit now that in spite of my misgivings about slow cookers as a student, as soon as I started fending for myself, I did find having one useful, but I confess to only making curries, casseroles and the occasional bean feast in my machine. But as my lifestyle changed over the years, my slow-cooking repertoire developed accordingly, and today I'm delighted to report that over the years I've discovered that there's an awful lot more to cook in a slow cooker than a casserole. And I'm not the only one who's cottoned on: quite by chance, when I first started writing this book, my sister-in-law Sarah (a 30-something, busy working mum of two) decided she would like a slow cooker for her birthday (and honestly, I had nothing to do with it!). After doing her research and selecting the model she wanted, she found out that she had to go on a waiting list because recent demand for slow cookers was so high that her local shop had sold out!

It would seem that this countertop appliance of yesteryear is indeed making a real impression upon us once again. No doubt it's got something to do with our continuing quest to save money where we can, but using the slow cooker makes sense in many other ways. Yes, you can be kind to your purse by buying cheap cuts of meat and stewing them tender in the cooker – the most celebratory of celebrity chefs have put traditional butchery cuts back on their menus because they taste so good and they've helped make it trendy to cook the same way our grandmothers used to. But equally appealing, if not more so, a slow cooker uses less energy while it's working, so it puts a big tick in our 'green' box too. More good news still, the slow cooker frees up more time for a life outside the kitchen, and food cooked in it retains plenty of nutrients, is packed full of flavour, and is deliciously tender and succulent to boot. The slow cooker is very versatile and there are plenty of different types of meal you can cook, some that will take several hours to cook, while others will cook in only a fraction of the time you might expect, so you should be able to find something to suit your lifestyle. Last but not least, you won't end up with a steamy, hot kitchen (it's great for cooking in the warmer months of the year too) and you'll only have one main cooking pot to wash once your meal is served up!

Keeping all these points in mind, you'll be pleased to know that this is not going to be a fuddy-duddy cookbook full of dull dishes swimming in gravy. After the opening pages of helpful tips and techniques and all the information you need to know to get

started, you'll find 90 delicious recipes to help whet your appetite. I have included one or two old favourites, but mostly I've put the emphasis on contemporary flavours and ingredients, and I've tried to cover as many as possible of the different types of dishes you can make in your machine, from the light and healthy to the more indulgent and decadent. There are recipes using meat, game, poultry, fish, rice, pasta and vegetables. You'll find breakfast dishes that simmer away all night ready for you to wake up to the following morning; a selection of lighter and some more hearty soups; meals for every night of the week, as well as a chapter of recipes for special days or for when you're entertaining or celebrating. It's not all about savoury cooking either, you'll find a variety of puddings, bakes and preserves, and there's even a fruity hot toddy to round off the book.

I hope you'll soon feel inspired, like me, to think about cooking with your slow cooker in a different way and I hope that I am able to tempt you into making up some of the recipes from this book. On that note, all I have left to say is: 'Take it easy and happy cooking, the *slow* way!'

KATHRYN HAWKINS

PRINCIPLES OF SLOW COOKING

SLOW COOKER EVOLUTION

The slow cooker evolved in America out of an electric glazed brown cooking 'crock' or pot developed for cooking beans, called the Naxon Beanery. Another American company, Rival, bought Naxon, developed their idea, and in 1971 introduced the good people of the US to the Crock-Pot™ with the marketing slogan 'Cooks all day while the cook's away', its prime function being to save time in the kitchen. In the early 1970s, more and more women were going out to work, they had one eye on the purse strings and the other on the clock. They wanted to make sure their families weren't missing out on the 'homely' taste of freshly cooked food and were on the look-out for economical, effortless ways to achieve this. So popular was the Crock-Pot™ that its name is now used as the generic term for the slow cooker in the US. Outside of the US, the slow cooker was marketed under the name of Slo-Cooker™, and soon became one of a range of popular countertop electrical appliances, all aimed at the busy working woman who wanted to cook a nutritional meal for her family, with the minimum of fuss and effort on her part.

When slow cookers first appeared, they consisted of a chunky glazed round or oval ceramic lidded dish that sat inside a sturdy plastic-coated metal housing unit, and was thermostatically controlled. Today's models are basically the same but they're sleeker in design and the finish is often brushed or shiny steel with a clear lid, giving them a more contemporary look. A Canadian friend of mine still has one of the original 1970s models, and in some respects the brown and orange colour scheme makes it collectably kitsch and just as attractive as some of the more recent digital cookers!

HOW A SLOW COOKER COOKS

The basic method behind cooking in this countertop electrical appliance is very simple. A thermostatically controlled electric heating element maintains a relatively low temperature (low compared to other cooking methods like baking, boiling and frying) for many hours, allowing the user to leave the cooker unattended. Liquid in some form is an essential part of the way a slow cooker cooks food, and because of this it is not possible to brown food or obtain a crust using a slow cooker. A thermostat ensures safety and permits the user to leave the cooker on without the fear of it overheating.

The slow cooker appliance consists of a lidded cooking pot surrounded by housing, usually metal, which contains the heating element usually in the bottom and sometimes up the sides of the cooker. The pot acts as a cooking container and a heat reservoir. The lid is usually transparent heatproof glass which sits on a rim around the pot edge. During cooking, condensed water vapour collects between the rim and the edge of the lid, and creates a low-pressure seal – you'll often hear the lid jolting on top of the cooker dish as the water bubbles form the seal. Unlike the pressure cooker, there is no build-up or difference in air pressure during cooking, making this a completely safe way to cook.

Cookers have different heat settings and thus use variable amounts of electricity, although in comparison to other kitchen appliances, output (wattage) is much lower. Typically, a slow cooker operates on an output of between 200 W and approximately 330 W at its highest setting. The slow cookers of old did not have changeable temperature controls and the contents could only be cooked on full heat; the length of time a dish could be set for cooking was often the only method of control. Precise cooking temperature varies according to the output of the machine but the usual range is from 62.7 to 93°C (145 to 200°F), depending on the setting. Harmful bacteria in food becomes dormant over 60°C (140°F) and is destroyed at 74°C (165°F), so as long as the food is cooked for the correct length of time, these temperatures will be reached and the food will be safe to eat. You'll often see the liquid or sauce bubbling away around the sides of the cooking pot, while the food towards the centre of the pot

remains at a gentler rate of cooking – this is quite normal. If you are in any doubt about the temperature of your cooked dish, it is advisable to use an external food probe or thermometer (see additional notes on food safety on pages 10–11).

Sometimes the cooker is preheated before ingredients are put in the pot, and most recipes call for hot liquid to be added; these two factors help the heating up process get started – important for 'high-risk' food such as poultry. Once the lid is put on the dish, the cooker is switched to the appropriate setting. During cooking, the liquid transfers heat from the pot walls to its contents. The lid is a very important

part of the appliance as it prevents liquid and heat from escaping – if it is removed or disturbed during cooking, the internal temperature will be affected. As cooking continues, the cooking liquid gets hotter and condenses into vapour, the lid is held on to the cooker dish by a form of suction which helps retain a moist cooking atmosphere. After a specified time, the food should be cooked to perfection.

SLOW-COOKED FOOD

Slow cooking is a very nutritious way to cook food. When food is cooked by traditional methods like boiling, water-soluble vitamins and antioxidants leach out into the cooking water and can escape in the steam. During slow cooking, while some nutrients do escape in the cooking liquid as it condenses around the edge of the lid, most are retained in the cooking juices because the cooking pot and lid create a sealed unit. This is one of the reasons why it is important not to remove the lid during the cooking process, unless absolutely necessary. More flavours are retained too, and in a greater concentration, so much so that you may find that you need to reduce the quantity of seasonings and flavours you add to your cooking.

One slight drawback of this cooking system is that as well as the liquid, fat is also retained and doesn't reduce down. You'll need to trim as much excess fat as you can from any meat before you put it in the slow cooker, and try to restrict the use of fatty ingredients as much as possible. Sometimes this is unavoidable and you may end up with a layer of fat on top of the finished dish, but you can either skim it off using a flat spoon, or try blotting the top gently with absorbent kitchen paper. If you have more time, make the dish up the day before serving it, transfer it to another heatproof container to cool

completely, then cover and chill overnight. The next day, any fat will have solidified on top of the dish and you'll be able to remove it easily before reheating the food thoroughly (see page 16).

Some foods do not take well to conventional, quick-cooking methods, especially cheaper cuts of meat with gristly bits and chunky, lean muscle fibre – cuts from the part of the animal that work hard like the neck, legs and shoulder. If these are cooked at too high a temperature or for insufficient time, they will be tough and chewy. These cuts of meat need long, slow cooking with plenty of moisture or cooking liquid in order to 'melt' the tougher parts and soften up the meaty muscle. These cuts are often the tastiest, and the slow cooker is the perfect way to cook them. Good news still, these cuts of meat are relatively cheap, so look out for brisket, shin, skirt, flank, hock and scrag end of neck: the slow cooker will tenderize them to perfection.

SOME IMPORTANT FOOD SAFETY TIPS

While slow cooking is a very safe way to cook most types of food, there are a few considerations to take into account when preparing specific foods. Raw kidney beans and some other beans like soya beans, contain a toxin which is usually destroyed by rapid boiling for ten minutes prior to the start of cooking. The slow cooker cannot perform this function as it won't reach a high enough temperature quickly enough, so you'll need to pre-boil beans and some other pulses before you put them in the slow cooker dish in order to destroy the toxin. You will also need to pre-soak most beans and pulses overnight before cooking as directed. Alternatively, use canned equivalents and add them for the last hour or so of cooking to heat them though.

Slow cookers do not provide sufficient heat to compensate for loss of moisture and heat if you keep taking the lid off, for example, if you need to keep adding ingredients to a specific recipe. Slow cooker recipes are designed for mostly uninterrupted cooking in order to keep the temperature constant for even, safe cooking and maximum moisture retention. It can take up to 20 minutes for the cooker to reheat again after the lid has been removed. If you are adding ingredients to the cooker, you must give them time to cook or heat through thoroughly before the food can be eaten to avoid the danger of food-poisoning bacteria formation. Avoid adding frozen ingredients to your cooker as these will lower the cooking temperature too drastically. Minimal quantities of small frozen ingredients like peas, berries, chopped herbs and diced vegetables are fine to add once the main cooking is underway, but you'll need to add extra time to ensure they cook properly. Other factors can also affect the heating capability of your cooker, such as power surges or low voltage, an extremely cold external temperature, or positioning the cooker in a draught or by an open window. If any of these conditions are unavoidable, adjust the cooking time accordingly to ensure thorough cooking.

Large pieces of pork and ham and all poultry should be put in a preheated slow cooker and cooked on High for at least 1 to 2 hours to accelerate cooking. After this time, the setting can be switched to Low for longer, slower cooking, if preferred. A meat thermometer or food probe is a worthwhile investment if you're planning to cook large cuts of meat in your cooker. It is the most reliable way to ensure that the inside of the meat has reached a high enough temperature to destroy any potentially harmful bacteria.

COOKING TIMES

When it comes to determining how long something will take to cook, usually you will see cooking times in recipe books given as, for example, '6–8 hours on Low'. If you compare this to traditional cooking methods, you'll notice that this is a huge difference in time. In slow cooking recipes, this is quite permissible because it is a much more subtle means of cooking food and it is hard to overcook most things. The time differences equate to minimum and maximum times: after 6 hours the dish will be ready to eat if wanted immediately, but after a further 2 hours it will still be just as delicious. The time difference gives the cook more time to fit the meal around their other plans – the slow cooker is the perfect answer to the prayers of the disorganized cook who needs 'just a bit more time' to get everything ready at once!

To simplify timings, I give the cooking time in most instances as the time taken until the dish is completely cooked, and then as the reader, you will know that you have a little more time to get other things ready. There are a few recipes where the time given is a maximum time (in the breakfast section), and some where the timing is exact – fish, rice and pasta are some of the few foods which will overcook if left too long in the cooker. If you have a Keep Warm setting, you may wish to turn the cooker to this setting; it keeps most foods for up to 4 hours without them spoiling.

The cooking time of a dish on the High setting is just over half that of food cooked on the Low setting. On the Low setting you have up to 2 hours extra to add to the stated cooking time, and on the High setting you have up to 1 hour on top; on Keep Warm you have up to 4 hours. After these timings, the food will start to overcook, and the texture and flavour will suffer.

CHOOSING THE RIGHT MODEL FOR YOU

Slow cookers come in a variety of sizes, so choose a model to suit your personal requirements. You should find models ranging from 2 L (3½ pt) which will make enough food for two people, while at the other end of the spectrum a 6 L (10½ pt) cooker will serve a family of six. For testing the recipes in this book, I used a 4 L (7 pt) model which will serve up to four people. It is important not to over- or underfill a slow cooker, the heating elements being at the bottom and sometimes also partway up the sides, means that there is usually a minimum recommended liquid level to ensure even cooking, so you may need a slightly larger model than you first might think. As a general rule, avoid filling your cooker more than three-quarters full (2–3 cm / ¾–1¼ in) of the brim, but filling less than half-full will mean that food will cook too quickly and may dry out. Always check the manufacturer's recommendation for filling levels.

You will find round-dished models or oval ones. If you plan to make pot roasts or want to be able to cook in a loaf tin, an oval dish is preferable, while the round ones are better for casseroles and for taking small cake tins and pudding basins.

Different models have various temperature settings: Low, Medium, High and Keep Warm are the most usual. Some settings are controlled by means of a mechanical dial and have to be manually turned off, meaning that the cook has to be present at the end of cooking time. More sophisticated models are digital. Digital cooker settings tend to be more accurate and can sometimes be pre-programmed in advance for extended or delayed cooking (the latter is not recommended for raw meat). The most advanced cookers have computerized timing devices that allow the cook to program the cooker to perform multiple operations (e.g. 2 hours on High, followed by 2 hours on Low, followed by Keep Warm for a further specified time).

Always refer to the manufacturer's guide for information on settings but, in general, the settings vary the temperature during cooking to improve the flavour and texture of the food and help avoid overcooking. Think about the types of dishes and the foods you want to cook before choosing a model. The High setting is for quicker cooking and is used with poultry, pork, cakes and egg-based dishes as it heats up the food more quickly; the Low setting is used for longer, slower cooking, such as tenderizing tougher cuts of meat. Keep Warm does exactly that, without drying out the food. The Medium setting is usually 1 hour on High followed by an indefinite time at a reduced medium heat. The recipes in this book call for the Low and High settings only.

You will also find slow cookers set within other appliances, such as a rice cooker or steamer. Such '3-in-1' machines have limited slow cooking settings but of course, offer other functions instead. Some of the latest slow cookers have a built-in sauté pan which allows the user to brown meat and vegetables within the appliance instead of a frying pan before the slow cooking begins. Choosing a specific appliance is a case of personal preference and it is usually your budget and storage space that determine just how many individual appliances you can fit in your kitchen.

In terms of output, most traditional slow cookers use between 200 W and 330 W, which in terms of the modern home is the equivalent of a few light bulbs – a mere smidgen of the electricity used by more conventional cooking machines.

WHAT YOUR SLOW COOKER CAN COOK FOR YOU

The range of foods you can cook in a slow cooker is extremely diverse and whatever you choose will be full of flavour and all the nutritional value that this way of cooking preserves. Below is a list of foods ideal for slow cooking.

Meat: tender, leans cuts like beef fillet, lamb noisettes and pork loin chops, or any cut you'd consider for stir-frying, grilling or pan-frying *are not* best suited to long, slow cooking. Instead, choose cuts for roasting or casseroling – check out the traditional cuts, such as brisket, shin, skirt, flank and hock; they're not only very tasty but they're cheap too. Have a look at mutton – it's been making a come-back in recent years and is perfect for the slow cooker. Always trim away as much excess fat from meat as possible before cooking to avoid greasy gravies and sauces. Minced meat is usually made up from a variety of meat cuts, and cooks well made into burgers, balls or as part of a soup or stew. Good-quality meaty sausages are fine for slow cooking – you'll need to brown them first, and expect the texture to be softer than fried, roasted or grilled ones.

Poultry and game: all cuts of chicken are suitable for slow cooking. If you're leaving the skin on, it is better to brown it first, otherwise it will look very pale. For food safety's sake, poultry is always cooked or started off on the High setting. Obviously, a whole turkey won't fit in a slow cooker, but prepared turkey joints and other cuts are fine. A whole duck is too fatty, but the meat is very good for lengthy cooking. Choose duck joints instead, or use skinned duck meat and cook it as part of a casserole. Goose is not suitable as it is too fatty. Small game birds are perfect for pot-roasting and casseroles, and can be left whole or jointed. Furred game, such as rabbit, hare and venison is also suitable for pot roasts, stews and casseroles.

Fish and shellfish: using a slow cooker for cooking fish is one of the best ways to enjoy its delicate flavour and texture. When it comes to shellfish, large, live specimens, such as lobster or crab are too big to cook quickly enough in a slow cooker, but providing the cooking sauce is sufficiently cooked and hot, raw peeled or whole

prawns, baby clams and mussels cook very well on the High setting. Otherwise, it is best to add cooked, defrosted shellfish towards the end of cooking so that it stays moist and succulent. All fish is best served as soon as it is cooked to enjoy its succulent texture. Squid is an exception as it benefits from the slow, moist cooking of this method, and can be used fresh and raw right from the beginning of cooking time. It can also be kept warm on a holding setting.

Vegetables: there are very few vegetables that are best left out of the slow cook's repertoire, and these are delicate varieties that are easy to spoil, such as asparagus and globe artichokes (although cooked or canned prepared chopped spears or hearts can be added to sauces towards the end of cooking time). The colour, texture and delicate flavours of these vegetables when fresh would soon diminish in slow cooking.

Flavourings: when you first start cooking with your slow cooker you'll probably find that the natural flavours of the ingredients you put in your recipes are more prominent. This is because conventional cooking often 'cooks out' some of the flavours in steam and cooking water. You'll find that food from your slow cooker is far from bland and you may end up using less seasoning and additional flavourings than you would do normally. Some herbs have a delicate fragrance and texture which can be lost in the prolonged cooking, but robust herbs like rosemary, bay, sage and thyme hold up well. Soft-leaved herbs like dill, coriander, basil, tarragon and parsley are better added towards the end of cooking time or just before eating. Dried herbs are a good choice for slow cooking, but remember their flavour is more concentrated so a little goes a long way. Spices can be added at the beginning of cooking as you would normally, but it is worth experimenting by using less than usual to avoid too dominant a flavour – for prolonged cooking, whole spices are a better choice than ground because they are mellower and have a tendency to be less pungent. Other seasonings, such as ketchups, condiments, pastes and extracts can be used in the slow cooker but remember that they often increase the salt and sugar content of a dish as well as adding flavour and richness.

Rice: choose 'easy-cook' varieties of rice for slow cooking which have been processed to ensure the grains remain separate once cooked. You'll find easy-cook varieties of long grain, brown and basmati rice. Easy-cook brown rice holds up well to lengthy cooking but other varieties quickly overcook and become very soft. Arborio (risotto) rice will cook fine in the slow cooker, but will soon overcook, so timing is just as important in the slow cooker as it is when cooking a risotto in a saucepan, but of course, you don't have to stand by the pan, stirring all the time! Cooked rice can also be used in the slow cooker and is best added towards the end of cooking time (final 30 minutes to 1 hour). Serve all rice dishes as soon after cooking as possible.

Pasta: standard dry and 'easy-cook' pastas can be cooked in the slow cooker but are not suitable for long cooking times as pasta quickly becomes soggy and flabby. Sometimes a recipe calls for pasta to be softened a little in boiling water before adding to the slow cooker (particularly larger pasta shapes). This will help the pasta absorb cooking liquid when added to the slow cooker so that it cooks more evenly. Fresh pasta, apart from lasagne sheets, is not recommended for slow cooking as it requires a lot of water to cook properly and it cooks much more quickly than dry varieties. Serve all pasta dishes as soon after cooking as possible.

Grains: pearl barley, quinoa, and whole wheat and rye grains can be cooked in the slow cooker. Some will require pre-soaking, so follow manufacturer's guidelines. For speedier cooking, pre-soak any grain to shorten the cooking time. These grains are more robust than rice and can withstand prolonged cooking.

Beans and pulses: as for conventional cooking, most beans and pulses require overnight soaking before they can be cooked – always follow recipe and manufacturer's guidelines. Some beans, especially kidney and soya beans, require rapid boiling for 10 minutes before adding to the slow cooker. Canned or cooked pulses can be used in slow cooking and should be added according to the recipe.

Fruit: any fruit that you would normally cook is perfect for slow cooking, in fact, some are better cooked this way as the gentle cooking helps prevent fruit pieces breaking up as they soften and tenderize.

Dairy: milk, cream and similar products are not best suited to prolonged cooking as they begin to break up and separate, spoiling the appearance and texture of a dish. If you are planning on cooking for a lengthy period of time, add these ingredients towards the end of cooking time (final 30 minutes to 1 hour). Serve dairy-rich dishes as soon after cooking as possible.

Sugar: as with dairy, sugar doesn't withstand lengthy cooking either and starts to concentrate and caramelize, thus spoiling the flavour and appearance of a dish. This applies mostly when sugar is used in great quantity in a dish, but adding liquid will help counteract the problem.

REHEATING

Casseroles, soups and stews are often cooked the day before eating as their flavour improves with keeping and reheating, and also helps reduce the fat content of a dish (see page 10). If you are planning to reheat something you've made, you must make sure you follow a few golden rules. Once the dish has finished cooking in the slow cooker, remove the ceramic dish from the slow cooker unit and stand on a heat-resistant mat or stand. Remove the lid and cool for 10 minutes before transferring the

contents to a heatproof dish. Leave to cool completely, then cover and chill. It is not advisable to reheat food in your slow cooker as it takes too long to reach the correct temperature. Therefore, it is safer to reheat the dish by conventional means like a saucepan on the hob. For safety, meat dishes should come to a gentle simmer for at least 30 minutes to ensure the meat is thoroughly heated.

For a quick eco tip, the slow cooker is a great way to heat up cooked bread rolls. Just pop them in the cooker, cover with the lid, switch on to High and leave for at least 25 minutes to warm through. It's a much greener alternative to putting on a conventional oven or grill.

FINISHING TOUCHES

One of the significant differences with slow cooker cooking is that food does not brown due to the high moisture content. In order to give some types of food like meat more of an appetizing appearance, it is often suggested that meat is 'browned' before you put it in the cooker; sausages, chicken and cubed meat all benefit from a little pan frying before being slow-cooked. Cakes and bakes steam rather than bake in the traditional sense, so they tend to be heavier in texture and don't develop the usual crust that would form if they were oven-baked. Dusting with sugar or adding a topping or icing after cooking will help give a more appealing finish. Cheese melts rather than crisps, so my solution for serving dishes where you want to emphasize cheese as an ingredient is to make toasted cheese discs under the grill which can be placed on top of each serving, giving an authentic cheesy crust. Toasted breadcrumbs also make a good alternative to a toasted or grilled crust on a finished dish and add a crisp texture. Most simple of all is to sprinkle your finished dish with some chopped fresh herbs to add a splash of colour and a fresh taste. Please remember that unless otherwise stated, it is not safe to put the slow cooker dish in a conventional oven or under a grill in order to brown the top.

Because most of the liquid you add to a slow cooker is retained, you may find that the contents are a bit too sloppy or that the sauce is too thin. Avoid draining off this nutrient-rich gravy – it is better to make it more palatable by thickening it up. All you need to do is make a smooth paste from 1 tablespoon of cornflour blended with 2 tablespoons of cold water per approximately 450 ml (¾ pt) of liquid. About 30 minutes to 1 hour before the end of cooking time, stir it into the contents of your dish, re-cover and continue to cook to thicken up the juices.

CONVERTING YOUR OWN RECIPES FOR SLOW COOKER COOKING

It's pretty straightforward to cook your favourite conventional method recipes in a slow cooker. You do need to bear in mind that the temperature of your slow cooker, even on its highest setting, is still cooler than the lowest setting in a conventional oven – as a general rule, casseroles of meat and vegetables take up to 8 hours on the Low setting. Less liquid is required for slow cooking as little is lost during the cooking process, so you may need to reduce the quantity you add by as much as half if necessary. You may also wish to use a little less flavourings such as chilli, garlic, herbs, spices and other seasonings, as flavours are more concentrated in the slow cooker. If at the end of cooking the food is not quite ready, increase the setting to High and cook in 30-minute sessions until the food is thoroughly cooked.

GETTING STARTED: SLOW COOKING TIPS AND TECHNIQUES

Here are a few general do's and don'ts to help you get the most from your slow cooker. You should always read the booklet that comes with your machine, as instructions often vary between manufacturers:

Before you start cooking, make sure your cooker is on a heatproof, level surface where it will be safe from accidents – the kitchen countertop is ideal. The outside of the cooker gets quite hot with prolonged cooking as well as containing very hot food so make sure children and pets can't get anywhere near the cooker or its cable when it's being used. Allow space around the machine so that heat doesn't build up on another surface or appliance nearby.

A little bit of menu planning: have a good read through the recipe you want to cook to make sure you have sufficient time. With each recipe you'll see clearly at the start how long preparation should take, followed by the cooking involved, that way you can plan your meal to give yourself the least amount of work.

About the cooker dish: the dish supplied with the cooker is the only one intended for use with the rest of the cooker. Do not use the dish or lid if it is damaged or cracked as this will affect its cooking efficiency. Do not use the cooker dish in a microwave oven, in a conventional oven, on a hob or under the grill. Avoid putting a hot cooker dish on a wet or cold surface, or anything polished or with a special finish – use a heatproof mat or pot stand. The cooker dish will become very hot during cooking, so always use oven gloves or other heat protection when removing

it from the machine. Do not expose the cooker dish to extremes of temperature (like trying to cool a hot pot by running cold water over it) as it may crack. Make sure the pot is at room temperature or gently warmed (rinsing it with warm water) before adding hot ingredients to it. It is not advisable to use the slow cooker dish as a storage container in the fridge, unless otherwise stated.

During cooking: unless stated in a recipe, do not be tempted to lift the lid during cooking as this will lower the temperature and will alter the cooking time. If you can see the contents drying out, add sufficient hot liquid and keep the lid off for as short a time as possible. Add between 10 and 20 minutes to the cooking time per lid lift, depending on how long it is removed each time. Take care when removing the lid, particularly if foil is used as well, as steam will escape and could scald (see Coverings).

After cooking: make sure that the food is thoroughly hot before serving, then either turn the control to Warm to keep food hot for up to 4 hours (no longer), or switch the cooker control to Off, and turn off at the mains. Stir the contents if appropriate before serving to ensure a good mix of flavours and ingredients. Allow the appliance and the pot to cool completely before cleaning.

Cleaning and storing: wash the cooking dish in warm soapy water. Any dried-on food can be removed using a rubber spatula, a cleaning sponge or a cloth – avoid anything abrasive. Check the manufacturer's instructions as some cooker dishes can be washed in the dishwasher. The lid is usually washed by hand only. Make sure both dish and lid are well dried before fitting back in the housing unit. The cooker housing unit must not be immersed in water. For general cleaning, wipe the body of the cooker using a damp, soft cloth and a little mild detergent but make sure all traces of the detergent are wiped off with a clean cloth, and dry thoroughly before heating up again. As with most kitchen appliances, it is safest to store your slow cooker fully assembled, with the cable neatly tied up.

Using other containers within your slow cooker dish: sometimes a recipe requires a specific size tin, bowl or dish. This is usually for cakes, puddings, pâtés and terrines, and some preserves. Make sure the dish required is heatproof and that it fits inside the cooker with the lid on. Some recipes require a water bath, or *bain marie*, and may recommend that the dish stands on a trivet, in order to create a steam bath. If you don't have a trivet, use an upturned heatproof saucer or a large metal pastry cutter as a stand. Check that the lid of the cooker still fits properly otherwise steam will escape and no cooking seal will be possible. Unless otherwise stated, pour hot (not boiling) water into your slow cooker dish – this helps maintain the correct cooking temperature and doesn't risk cracking the dish with sudden extreme heat.

If you want to make a reduced quantity of a recipe (say for 1 or 2 people), you can put the appropriate amount in a smaller, heatproof dish which can then be placed inside the main slow cooker dish. Make sure the cooker lid still fits on top, and then pour in sufficient hot water in the main cooker dish to come halfway up the sides of the smaller dish. Cover and cook as directed – reduced quantities may take up to 1 hour less than the stated cooking time.

Coverings: sometimes a recipe may suggest covering the food in your slow cooker with extra protection as well as the lid. This will hasten up the cooking time of specific ingredients like onions or help prevent drying out when little or no liquid is used (pot-roasting). Put a layer of foil, shiny-side down (for maximum heat retention), on top of the slow cooker dish and sit the lid on top, pressing it down on the rim to ensure it sits completely flat. Take care when removing this foil layer as there is likely to be a blast of scalding steam.

Occasionally, covering food is also required to protect some mixtures from the moisture which collects on the lid when a water bath is used; the covering also helps to provide an extra heat pocket to help the mixture cook evenly and quickly. Most mixtures expand during cooking, e.g. cake mixes rise as their raising agents begin to work, and egg mixtures also expand as they set, so you need to ensure that you make room for the mixture to rise as well as making sure it is being protected. Above all else, you need to make sure that there is sufficient room to allow the mixture to rise beneath the slow cooker lid to avoid it being lifted and the seal being broken. For an effective covering of a soft mixture such as a cake batter, cut a piece of baking parchment 2.5 cm (1 in) larger than the top of the selected cooking dish, and using scissors, snip 1 cm (½ in) all the way round at short intervals to create a foldable edge. Sit the parchment directly on top of the mixture, making sure that the top of the mixture is completely covered and that the foldable edge sits snugly against the side of the cooking dish. For extra protection, loosely cover the top of the dish with foil to allow room for the mixture to rise, and seal tightly round the edge of the dish to ensure it is watertight. If the rise on a mixture is great, pleat the centre of the foil before securing it to the top of the dish.

RECIPES

SWEET AND FRAGRANT FRUIT **COMPOTE**

There are so many different dried fruits available to buy now, you'll be able to make up your own combination of favourites. Serve this hot or cold with yoghurt.

PREPARATION
5 minutes

COOKING TIME
overnight
(up to 9 hours) on Low

SERVES 4–6

150 g (5½ oz) ready-to-eat dried apricots
150 g (5½ oz) dried apple rings
50 g (2 oz) dried cranberries
1 unwaxed lemon
1 cinnamon stick, broken
6 cardamom pods, lightly crushed
Natural yoghurt (optional), to serve

1 Rinse all the dried fruit in a colander, shake off the excess water and transfer to the slow cooker dish.

2 Using a vegetable peeler, pare off three long strips of lemon rind into the fruit. Extract the juice and pour it into the dish.

3 Pour over 900 ml (1½ pt) cold water to cover the fruit and add the spices.

4 Cover with the lid, switch the cooker on to Low, and leave to cook overnight or for up to 9 hours. Discard the spices and lemon rind.

5 To serve, spoon the compote into serving bowls and top with a dollop of thick yoghurt, if liked. Delicious served with hot cinnamon toast (see Cook's note). Alternatively, allow to cool and chill for at least 1 hour before serving.

COOK'S NOTE

For cinnamon toast, just before serving your compote, preheat the grill to a hot setting, and lightly toast four thick slices of white bread for 1 to 2 minutes on each side. Spread one side with a little softened butter and dust lightly with ground cinnamon and light brown sugar. Put back under the grill for a further 1 to 2 minutes until bubbling and hot.

BEANY VEGETABLE **HASH**

Get your taste buds up and running with this zingy concoction of vegetables and spices. You can omit the spices if preferred and change the amount of chilli to suit.

PREPARATION
15 minutes

COOKING TIME
5 minutes + overnight
(up to 9 hours) on Low

SERVES 4

450 g (1 lb) general-purpose potatoes
1 onion
1 green pepper
1 red pepper
2 red or green chillies
25 g (1 oz) butter
2 Tbsp vegetable oil

350 g (12½ oz) ripe tomatoes
400 g (14 oz) can pinto or kidney beans,
   drained and rinsed
1 tsp ground cumin
1 tsp paprika
Salt and freshly ground black pepper
2 Tbsp freshly chopped parsley

1 Peel the potatoes and cut into ½ cm (¼ in) cubes. Peel and finely chop the onion. Deseed and slice the peppers and chillies.

2 Melt the butter with the oil in a large frying pan until hot and bubbling and stir-fry all the prepared vegetables for 5 minutes. Transfer the vegetables to the slow cooker dish.

3 Quarter the tomatoes and mix into the vegetables, along with the kidney beans, cumin, paprika and plenty of seasoning. Cover with the lid, switch the cooker on to Low and leave to cook overnight or for up to 9 hours.

4 To serve, stir the hash well. Pile on to warm serving plates, sprinkle with chopped parsley and serve immediately.

COOK'S NOTE

If you like eggs for breakfast, serve this dish topped with a fried or poached egg, or make up an omelette, then shred into thin strips and fold into the mixture just before serving.

RISE-AND-SHINE BLUEBERRY **MUFFIN**

A cake-type muffin rather than the breaded sort, this bake makes a comforting and satisfying indulgent start to the day. Reminds me of hot cross buns. Mmm...

PREPARATION
25 minutes + cooling

COOKING TIME
overnight
(up to 10 hours) on Low

SERVES 4–6

175 g (6 oz) spelt or regular plain wholemeal flour
¾ tsp baking powder
1½ tsp ground mixed spice
75 g (2½ oz) caster sugar
75 g (2½ oz) butter or margarine, melted
2 medium eggs, beaten

100 ml (3½ fl oz) whole milk
Finely grated rind of 1 lemon
150 g (5½ oz) blueberries, plus extra to serve
50 g (2 oz) icing sugar
Approx 2 tsp lemon juice

1 Put an upturned saucer or large metal pastry cutter in the bottom of the slow cooker dish and pour in sufficient cold water to come 2.5 cm (1 in) up the sides of the dish. Grease and line a deep 15 cm (6 in) round cake tin – make sure the tin fits in your slow cooker.

2 Sieve the flour, baking powder and ground mixed spice into a mixing bowl and add any husks that remain in the sieve. Stir in the sugar and make a well in the centre. Add the melted butter or margarine and eggs, and mix in with the milk and lemon rind to form a thick batter.

3 Fold half the blueberries into the batter and spoon the mixture into the prepared tin. Smooth the top and sprinkle over the remaining blueberries. Cover the surface of the mixture completely with a circle of baking parchment (see page 19).

4 Stand the tin on the saucer or cutter. Cover with the lid and switch the cooker on to Low, and leave to cook overnight or for up to 9 hours.

5 Remove the tin from the cooker, discard the paper, and stand on a wire rack. Allow to cool for 30 minutes before removing the muffin from the tin.

6 Sift the icing sugar into a bowl and bind together with sufficient lemon juice to make a smooth, dropping consistency. Drizzle over the warm muffin before slicing and serve with extra blueberries, if liked.

COOK'S NOTE

To serve this mixture as a cake, follow step 1 but put the slow cooker on High to preheat for 20 minutes. Make up the mixture as directed and cover in the same way. Put the cake tin in the cooker dish, cover with the lid, and cook on 1½ hours until risen and firm to the touch. Remove from the cooker and cool completely on a wire rack before removing from the tin and icing as above.

A SLOW ENGLISH **BREAKFAST**

Sometimes it's nice to have a hearty breakfast as a treat once in a while, but cooking is something not all of us can face first thing in the morning. Let your slow cooker do it all for you and be delighted by the feast that awaits you.

 PREPARATION
10 minutes

COOKING TIME
4 minutes + overnight
(up to 9 hours) on Low

SERVES 4

4 beef tomatoes
250 g (9 oz) chestnut (brown) mushrooms
Salt and freshly ground black pepper
Few dashes of Worcestershire sauce
  (optional)

4 rashers rindless, thick-cut smoked
  bacon
8 good-quality thick pork or beef
  sausages
2 Tbsp vegetable oil

1 Wash and thickly slice the tomatoes. Wipe and halve the mushrooms. Arrange in the slow cooker dish in layers, seasoning well and adding a few dashes of Worcestershire sauce if liked.

2 Cut the bacon rashers in half lengthways and wrap one strip around each sausage. Heat the oil in a large frying pan and brown the sausages for 2 minutes, turn over and cook again for 2 minutes.

3 Arrange the sausages on top of the mushrooms and tomatoes, and drizzle over the pan juices. Cover with the lid, switch the cooker on to Low, and leave to cook overnight or for up to 9 hours.

4 To serve, using tongs, arrange the sausages on warm serving plates, then using a slotted spoon, drain the vegetables and pile on the plates. Serve immediately.

COOK'S NOTE

For a spicier start to the day, replace the Worcestershire sauce with a few drops of Tabasco or your favourite chilli sauce. Perfect served with hot buttered toast.

WINTER'S DAY **BRUNCH**

A much more decadent version of a cooked breakfast and, needless to say, very tasty and filling. The ideal set-you-up before a long country walk.

PREPARATION
15 minutes

COOKING TIME
7 minutes + overnight (up to 9 hours) on Low

SERVES 4

450 g (1 lb) general-purpose potatoes
1 onion
25 g (1 oz) butter
1 Tbsp vegetable oil
300 g (10½ oz) pork sausagemeat
40 g (1½ oz) porridge oats

1 tsp dried sage
Salt and freshly ground black pepper
175 g (6 oz) piece black pudding
4 large field or flat mushrooms
2 Tbsp freshly chopped parsley
Fresh tomatoes, to serve

1 Peel the potatoes, then cut into ½ cm (¼ in) cubes. Peel and finely chop the onion.

2 Melt the butter with the oil in a large frying pan until hot and bubbling, and stir-fry the potatoes and onion for 5 minutes. Using a slotted spoon, transfer the vegetables to the slow cooker dish. Reserve the pan juices.

3 Mix the sausagemeat with the oats, sage and a little seasoning, and form into four flattish patties. Cut the black pudding into four slices. Peel the mushrooms and slice thickly.

4 Reheat the pan juices until hot, and fry the sausage patties and black pudding slices for 1 minute on each side until lightly browned.

5 Mix the mushrooms into the potatoes and onion, and season well. Lay the sausage patties and black pudding on top, cover with the lid, switch the cooker on to Low, and leave to cook overnight or for up to 9 hours.

6 To serve, drain all the breakfast ingredients and pile on to warm serving plates. Sprinkle with chopped parsley and accompany with fresh tomatoes. Serve immediately.

COOK'S NOTE

For an even heartier breakfast, serve with creamy scrambled eggs on the side.

READY-FOR-BREAKFAST **PORRIDGE**

This is porridge made the traditional way, using pinhead oatmeal. Usually, you have to soak this coarsely ground oatmeal overnight and then cook it – here the slow cooker does it all for you. Use this method for cooking jumbo oats as well.

PREPARATION
2 minutes

COOKING TIME
overnight
(up to 10 hours) on Low

SERVES 4

1.1 L (2 pt) water or whole milk,
  or milk and water combined
175 g (6 oz) pinhead (coarse) oatmeal
Pinch of salt
2 Tbsp caster or light brown sugar,
  honey, maple syrup or golden syrup
  (optional)
Single cream or hot milk, to serve

1 Pour the water and/or milk into the slow cooker dish. Whisk in the oatmeal using a fork until well blended and season with a pinch of salt.

2 Cover with the lid, switch the cooker on to Low, and leave to cook overnight or for up to 10 hours, until thick and soft.

3 To serve, stir well and sweeten if preferred. Serve with single cream or hot milk for an extra indulgent start to the day.

COOK'S NOTE

Add chopped dried fruit and/or chopped nuts to the mix for a fruit-and-nut porridge, or stir chopped or mashed banana, grated apple or chopped fresh berries into freshly cooked porridge.

CHINESE CHICKEN AND VEGETABLE SOUP

A delicious light, colourful and fragrant soup. Add cooked noodles for the last 30 minutes of cooking for a more substantial dish.

PREPARATION
20 minutes

COOKING TIME
3 hours on High

SERVES 4

4 large chicken thighs
1 large carrot
1 garlic clove
1 large red pepper
2 star anise or 1 tsp Chinese
    five-spice powder
1 L (1¾ pt) hot good-quality chicken stock
150 g (5½ oz) baby corn

1 bunch of spring onions
150 g (5½ oz) small broccoli florets
115 g (4 oz) small shiitake or button
    mushrooms
1 Tbsp dark soy sauce
2 Tbsp Chinese cooking wine or dry sherry
4 Tbsp freshly chopped chives

1 Put the slow cooker on High to preheat for 20 minutes while you prepare the soup.

2 Remove the skin from the chicken thighs, wash and pat dry. Set aside. Peel and finely chop the carrot and garlic. Halve, deseed and finely chop the pepper.

3 Put the chicken in the slow cooker dish and add the carrot, pepper, garlic and star anise or five-spice powder. Pour over the hot stock, cover with the lid and leave to cook for about 2 hours until tender and the chicken falls off the bone.

4 While the chicken is cooking, trim the baby corn and slice thinly. Trim and chop the spring onions. Trim the broccoli and cut into small, even-sized pieces. Wipe and slice the mushrooms.

5 Carefully drain the chicken from the dish, and put the lid back on. Remove the bones from the chicken and shred the meat into strips. Return the chicken to the slow cooker, along with the prepared vegetables. Re-cover and continue to cook for a further hour. Discard the star anise, if using.

6 To serve, mix the soup well, stir in the soy sauce and wine or sherry. Ladle into warm serving bowls and sprinkle each with chopped chives.

COCK-A-LEEKIE-STYLE **BROTH**

A flavoursome chicken soupy-stew with tender grains of pearl barley – use
easy-cook white rice if preferred.

PREPARATION
20 minutes

COOKING TIME
5 minutes
+ 2 hours on High

SERVES 4

115 g (4 oz) pearl barley
4 large chicken thighs
4 rashers unsmoked streaky bacon
15 g (½ oz) butter
1 Tbsp vegetable oil

450 g (1 lb) leeks
1 bay leaf
1 L (1¾ pt) hot chicken stock
Salt and freshly ground black pepper
4 Tbsp freshly chopped chives

1 Put the slow cooker on High to preheat for 20 minutes while you prepare the broth. Rinse the pearl barley under cold running water and set aside.

2 Remove the skin from the chicken thighs, wash and pat dry. Cut the bacon into small pieces. Melt the butter with the oil in a frying pan until bubbling and hot, then fry the chicken and bacon for about 5 minutes, turning, until lightly browned. Set aside.

3 Trim the leeks. Split lengthways and rinse under cold running water to flush out any trapped earth. Shake well to remove excess water, then slice finely.

4 Put the pearl barley in the slow cooker dish. Pile the leeks on top and add the bay leaf. Arrange the chicken and bacon on top, along with all the pan juices. Pour over the hot stock and season well. Cover with the lid and leave to cook for about 2 hours until tender and the chicken falls off the bone. Remove the bones and bay leaf.

5 To serve, ladle into warm serving bowls and sprinkle each with chopped chives.

OLD-FASHIONED ON-THE-BONE HAM AND YELLOW PEA **SOUP**

Yellow split peas are a much-neglected pulse these days, but this soup is the perfect way to use them as they cook down to a soft, tender purée and absorb all the flavours of the ham.

PREPARATION
20 minutes

COOKING TIME
5 minutes
+ 2 hours on High
+ 2 hours on Low

SERVES 4

200 g (7 oz) dried yellow split peas, soaked overnight
900 g (2 lb) smoked ham hock, knuckle or shank, soaked overnight
1 medium onion
1 large carrot
1 stick celery

25 g (1 oz) butter
1 Tbsp vegetable oil
1 bay leaf
Freshly ground black pepper
1 L (1¾ pt) hot ham, chicken or vegetable stock
2 Tbsp freshly chopped parsley

1 Put the slow cooker on High to preheat for 20 minutes while you prepare the soup.

2 Drain and rinse the peas and the ham, and set aside. Peel the onion and carrot and chop finely. Trim and chop the celery. Melt the butter with the oil in a frying pan until bubbling and hot, then cook the vegetables, stirring, for 5 minutes to soften without browning. Stir in the yellow peas, add the bay leaf and season well with black pepper.

3 Spoon the vegetables into the slow cooker dish and sit the ham on top. Pour in the hot stock. Cover with the lid and cook for 2 hours, then turn the ham over, reduce the setting to Low, and continue to cook for a further 2 hours until the ham is so tender that it falls off the bone.

4 To serve, discard the bay leaf, and remove the skin and bone from the ham. Shred the meat finely and stir into the vegetables. Ladle into warm soup bowls and serve sprinkled with chopped parsley.

COOK'S NOTE

For a very smooth soup, blitz the vegetable mixture with a hand blender before adding the ham pieces.

CHILLI BEEF, TOMATO AND BEAN **SOUP**

This soup is so brimmed-full of ingredients that it's almost a meal in itself. Serve with a generous dollop of soured cream on top and tortilla chips or crusty bread to dunk.

PREPARATION
10 minutes
+ overnight soaking

COOKING TIME
18 minutes
+ 4 hours on High

SERVES 4

200 g (7 oz) dried black beans or
  kidney beans, soaked overnight
1 medium onion
250 g (9 oz) lean minced beef
1½ tsp hot chilli powder
1½ tsp ground cumin
1½ tsp dried thyme

400 g (14 oz) can chopped tomatoes
900 ml (1½ pt) hot beef stock
Salt and freshly ground black pepper
4 Tbsp freshly chopped coriander
4 Tbsp soured cream
Tortilla chips or crusty bread, to serve

1 Rinse and drain the beans. Put in a saucepan, cover with water and bring to the boil. Boil rapidly for 10 minutes (see Cook's note). Drain and put in the slow cooker dish.

2 Meanwhile, peel and finely chop the onion. Put the minced beef in a frying pan and heat gently, stirring for 1 to 2 minutes, until the juices begin to run. Stir in the onion and cook for 5 minutes, stirring regularly, until lightly browned. Add the spices, thyme and chopped tomatoes, and cook for a further minute.

3 Transfer to the slow cooker, pour over the stock and season well. Mix until well combined. Cover with the lid, switch the cooker on to High and leave to cook for about 4 hours until the beans are tender.

4 To serve, ladle into warm soup bowls, sprinkle with chopped coriander and top with a dollop of soured cream. Serve with tortilla chips or crusty bread.

COOK'S NOTE

Most dried beans and pulses require soaking overnight before cooking. After soaking, some dried beans also need to be thoroughly boiled for 10 minutes before slow cooking – this is due to the presence of a toxin in some beans, especially kidney beans; the boiling process helps destroy any possible harmful effects.

SMOKED HADDOCK AND RICE **CHOWDER**

All the flavours of the classic breakfast dish, kedgeree. The mild curried flavour blends perfectly with smoked fish.

PREPARATION
20 minutes

COOKING TIME
6 minutes
+ 1 hour on High

SERVES 4

1 medium onion
25 g (1 oz) butter
1 Tbsp mild curry paste
100 g (3½ oz) easy-cook white rice
900 ml (1½ pt) hot fish stock
1 bay leaf
350 g (12½ oz) skinless smoked
   haddock fillets

225 g (8 oz) frozen peas
4 Tbsp single cream
Salt and freshly ground black pepper
Few sprigs of fresh coriander,
   to garnish
Crusty bread, to serve

1 Put the slow cooker on High to preheat for 20 minutes while you prepare the chowder.

2 Peel and chop the onion. Melt the butter in a frying pan until bubbling and gently fry the onion with the curry paste for 5 minutes. Stir in the rice and cook for a further minute. Set aside.

3 Pour the hot stock into the slow cooker dish and mix in the rice and pan juices. Add the bay leaf. Cover with the lid and cook for 30 minutes. Add the fish fillets and frozen peas, re-cover and cook for a further 30 minutes, until the rice is tender and the fish flakes easily. Discard the bay leaf.

4 To serve, stir in the cream, taste and season. Ladle into warm serving bowls and sprinkle with extra black pepper if liked. Garnish with fresh coriander and serve with crusty bread.

COOK'S NOTE

For a healthier version, simply omit the cream.

'WAY DOWN SOUTH' PRAWN GUMBO

Based on a thick, spicy soup from the Louisiana region of the US. The sticky okra juices act as a mild thickening agent. If unavailable, replace with green beans.

PREPARATION
20 minutes

COOKING TIME
5 minutes
+ 1 hour 20 minutes
on High

SERVES 4

1 large onion
2 sticks celery with leaves
1 large green pepper
225 g (8 oz) okra
1 Tbsp vegetable oil
900 ml (1½ pt) hot fish or vegetable stock
100 g (3½ oz) easy-cook white rice

400 g (14 oz) can chopped tomatoes
2 bay leaves
Few sprigs of fresh thyme
350 g (12½ oz) large raw shelled prawns,
    thawed if frozen
Salt and freshly ground black pepper
Few drops of Tabasco sauce

1 Put the slow cooker on High to preheat for 20 minutes while you prepare the gumbo.

2 Peel and chop the onion. Reserving the celery leaves, trim and chop the stalks. Halve, deseed and chop the pepper. Trim and thickly slice the okra.

3 Heat the oil in a large frying pan and stir-fry the onion, celery and pepper for 5 minutes.

4 Pour the hot stock into the slow cooker dish and mix in the rice, vegetables and chopped tomatoes. Add the herbs. Cover with the lid and cook for 1 hour until the vegetables and rice are tender.

5 Stir in the prawns, re-cover and cook for a further 20 minutes, until the prawns are pink all over. Discard the herbs. Mix well and add seasoning and Tabasco sauce to taste.

6 To serve, wash and roughly chop the reserved celery leaves. Ladle the gumbo into warm bowls and sprinkle with the celery leaves.

COOK'S NOTE

If you don't like shellfish, either leave the prawns out altogether for a vegetarian dish or replace them with small pieces of cooked, lean chicken – add the chicken to the recipe at the same stage as you would the prawns.

ONION SOUP WITH WINE AND CHEESE

Using beef stock and red wine makes this onion soup tasty and very savoury.
For a less intense flavour, use vegetable stock and white wine instead.

⫴ PREPARATION
20 minutes

⚙ COOKING TIME
5 minutes
+ 4½ hours on High

⫲ SERVES 4

900 g (2 lb) onions
2 garlic cloves
25 g (1 oz) butter
1 Tbsp olive oil
2 tsp caster sugar
2 Tbsp plain flour
150 ml (¼ pt) dry red wine

1 L (1¾ pt) hot beef stock
2 sprigs of fresh rosemary
Salt and freshly ground black pepper
115 g (4 oz) Gruyère cheese, grated
2 Tbsp freshly chopped parsley
Toasted French bread and cut raw garlic
cloves, to serve

1 Put the slow cooker on High to preheat for 20 minutes while you prepare the soup.

2 Peel and finely slice the onions. Peel and chop the garlic. Melt the butter with the oil in a frying pan until bubbling, and gently fry the onions and garlic for 5 minutes to soften slightly.

3 Transfer the fried onions and pan juices to the slow cooker dish and arrange evenly. Cover the top of the dish with a layer of foil, shiny-side down, and then cover with the lid. Cook for 2 hours, stirring after an hour, until pale golden in colour.

4 Stir in the sugar, cover as before, and continue to cook for about 1½ hours, stirring after 40 minutes, until richly golden and tender.

5 Stir in the flour and gradually blend in the wine and stock. Add the rosemary and plenty of seasoning. Re-cover with just the lid and cook for 1 hour. Discard the rosemary.

6 To serve, stir the cheese into the soup and immediately ladle into warm soup bowls. Sprinkle with chopped parsley. Serve accompanied with toasted French bread rubbed with raw garlic.

COOK'S NOTE

Putting a layer of foil below the lid of the slow cooker helps the cooker retain a maximum amount of heat and moisture when no liquid is added. It is an excellent method for cooking down vegetables such as onions to a melting tenderness. Take care when removing the foil as the steam will be scalding.

MOROCCAN **CHICKPEA SOUP**

A very tasty, heart-warming soup that can be served as a light meal. Spoon over freshly steamed couscous or boiled rice.

PREPARATION
10 minutes + standing

COOKING TIME
5 minutes
+ 3 hours on Low

SERVES 4

1 large onion
2 garlic cloves
2.5 cm (1 in) piece root ginger
2 Tbsp olive oil
½–1 tsp dried chilli flakes
1 small cinnamon stick, broken
Pinch of saffron strands
900 ml (1½ pt) hot vegetable stock
400 g (14 oz) can chopped tomatoes

2 x 420 g (15 oz) cans chickpeas,
   drained and rinsed
Salt and freshly ground black pepper
½ small preserved lemon, seeds
   removed and finely chopped (see
   Cook's note)
4 Tbsp freshly chopped coriander
Toasted pita or naan bread, to serve

1   Put the slow cooker on High to preheat for 20 minutes while you prepare the soup.

2   Peel and chop the onion. Peel and finely chop the garlic and ginger. Heat the oil in a frying pan and gently fry the onion, garlic and ginger for 5 minutes to soften slightly.

3   Transfer to the slow cooker dish and mix in chilli flakes to taste and the spices. Pour over half the hot stock. Cover the top of the dish with a layer of foil, shiny-side down, and then cover with the lid. Cook for 1 hour until the onion is soft.

4   Reheat the remaining stock, and stir it in, along with the tomatoes and chickpeas, and plenty of seasoning. Re-cover with just the lid and cook for a further 2 hours, then stir in the lemon and chopped coriander. Re-cover, switch off the cooker, and leave to stand for 30 minutes to allow the flavours to develop. Discard the cinnamon stick.

5   To serve, ladle into warm soup bowls and serve with lightly toasted pita or naan bread.

COOK'S NOTE

Preserved lemons are a Moroccan speciality. Small lemons are pickled in brine and offer a sour piquancy when chopped and added to a variety of dishes. If unavailable, stir in the juice and finely grated rind of 1 small fresh lemon as indicated above.

AUTUMNAL PUMPKIN, SWEETCORN AND APPLE **SOUP**

Intensely golden in colour and full of earthy sweet flavours, this soup really defines the season. Curry spices also work well in this recipe.

PREPARATION
15 minutes

COOKING TIME
5 minutes
+ 5 hours on Low

SERVES 4

1 kg (2 lb 3 oz) pumpkin or squash
1 large onion
1 Tbsp cold-pressed rapeseed oil
  or other vegetable oil
1½ tsp ground ginger
1 tsp ground cumin

900 ml (1½ pt) hot vegetable stock
450 g (1 lb) Bramley cooking apples
1 Tbsp light brown sugar
Salt and freshly ground black pepper
175 g (6 oz) cooked sweetcorn kernels
2 tsp cumin seeds, lightly toasted

1 Slice off the skin from the pumpkin and remove the seeds. Cut into thin pieces about ½ cm (¼ in) thick and put in the slow cooker dish.

2 Peel and chop the onion. Heat the oil in a frying pan and fry the onion for 5 minutes until slightly softened. Mix into the pumpkin, along with the ground spices.

3 Pour over the hot stock, cover with the lid and switch the cooker on to Low. Cook for 3 hours until just tender. Meanwhile, peel, core and chop the apples. Add to the pumpkin along with the sugar and plenty of seasoning. Cover again and cook for a further 2 hours until very tender.

4 To serve, blitz with a hand blender until smooth, then stir in the sweetcorn. Taste and adjust the seasoning if necessary. Ladle into warm soup bowls and serve immediately sprinkled with toasted cumin seeds.

COOK'S NOTE

Use diced parsnip or sweet potato for an even sweeter version of this soup, or half pumpkin and half parsnip.

TANDOORI-STYLE CHICKEN AND FRESH MANGO 'CHUTNEY'

Traditionally, tandoori dishes are dry-roasted in a clay oven, but the slow cooker can give you just as tender and tasty a result. I prefer this dish served cold with a salad because it develops even more flavours on cooling.

PREPARATION
20 minutes

COOKING TIME
2 hours on High

SERVES 4

FOR THE CHICKEN
4 large skinless, boneless chicken thighs
Salt and freshly ground black pepper
1 garlic clove
2.5 cm (1 in) piece root ginger
1 green chilli
6 Tbsp whole milk natural yoghurt
1 Tbsp tomato purée
2 tsp Madras curry paste

FOR THE SALSA
1 ripe medium-size mango
1 green chilli
2 Tbsp freshly chopped mint
2 Tbsp white wine vinegar
1 Tbsp clear honey
Few black onion seeds (optional)
Grilled naan bread, to serve
Mint sprigs, to garnish

1 Put the slow cooker on High to preheat for 20 minutes while you prepare the chicken.

2 Wash and pat dry the chicken. Prick all over with a fork and place in a shallow dish. Season well.

3 Peel the garlic and ginger and finely chop. Place in a small bowl. Deseed and finely chop the chilli and mix into the garlic and ginger, along with the yoghurt, tomato purée and curry paste. Brush all over the chicken – for a more intense flavour, cover and chill for 2 hours before cooking.

4 Line the inside of the cooker dish with baking parchment and arrange the chicken pieces on top. Cover with the lid and cook for 2 hours, until the chicken is tender and cooked through (the internal temperature should read 80°C/176°F using a food probe). Drain well and place on a warm serving platter.

5 Just before serving, prepare the salsa. Slice the mango either side of the smooth, central flat stone and remove the skin. Finely chop the flesh and place in a serving bowl. Deseed and finely chop the chilli, and mix into the mango, along with the chopped mint, vinegar, honey and some seasoning. Set aside until ready to serve.

6 Serve the chicken hot or cold, sprinkled with black onion seeds, if liked. Accompany with the mango salsa and grilled naan bread. Garnish with mint sprigs.

TANGY BEEF AND SWEETCORN **LOAF**

At one time, meatloaf was a classic family favourite, now it's time to put it back on the menu and enjoy an updated version.

PREPARATION
20 minutes + standing

COOKING TIME
4 hours on Low

SERVES 4

1 bunch of spring onions
1 garlic clove
675 g (1½ lb) lean minced beef
75 g (2½ oz) fresh white breadcrumbs
4 Tbsp sweet chilli dipping sauce
2 Tbsp dark soy sauce
115 g (4 oz) cooked sweetcorn kernels
1 large egg, beaten
2 Tbsp freshly chopped coriander

1 Put an upturned saucer or large metal pastry cutter in the bottom of the slow cooker dish and pour in sufficient hot water to come 2.5 cm (1 in) up the sides of the dish. Switch the cooker on to High to preheat for 20 minutes while you prepare the meat loaf. Lightly grease a 900 g (2 lb) loaf tin – make sure the tin fits in your slow cooker.

2 Trim and chop the white and green parts of the spring onions and place in a mixing bowl. Peel and crush the garlic into the bowl. Break up the minced beef and put it in the bowl, along with the breadcrumbs, 2 tablespoons of the chilli dipping sauce, 1 tablespoon of the soy sauce and the sweetcorn. Mix well together, then bind with the egg.

3 Form into a smooth, firm mixture and fit neatly inside the prepared tin, pressing down gently. Cover the top of the tin with oiled foil, shiny-side down, and stand the tin on the saucer or cutter. Cover with the lid, reduce the setting to Low, and cook for 4 hours until the juices run clear. Remove from the cooker.

4 Mix the remaining chilli sauce and soy sauce together. Remove the foil from the loaf and pour the chilli mixture over the top. Cover up loosely and stand for 10 minutes before removing from the tin. Serve hot or cold in thick slices, sprinkled with chopped coriander.

COOK'S NOTE

If preferred, replace the chilli sauce with tomato ketchup.

BEEFY MUSHROOM AND BACON **BURGERS**

Large, flat mushrooms have a meaty texture, so by filling them with a classic hamburger mixture you can use less meat and still serve up a hearty burger.

PREPARATION
20 minutes

COOKING TIME
2½ hours on Low

SERVES 4

4 x 7–10 cm (3–4 in) diameter field
or flat mushrooms
1 small onion
225 g (8 oz) lean minced beef
1 Tbsp freshly chopped thyme
or 1 tsp dried

2 Tbsp chilli tomato ketchup,
plus extra to serve
4 rashers rindless smoked streaky
bacon
4 burger buns
Handful of assorted baby salad leaves

1 Put the slow cooker on High to preheat for 20 minutes while you prepare the burgers.

2 Peel the mushrooms and remove the stalks. Chop the stalks finely and put in a mixing bowl. Peel and finely chop the onion and put in the bowl, along with the beef and thyme. Mix well, then bind together with the ketchup.

3 Divide the mixture into four equal portions and shape each into a round burger shape to fit snugly inside each mushroom. Wrap a rasher of bacon around each.

4 Line the bottom of the slow cooker dish with baking parchment and arrange the stuffed mushrooms, side by side, seam-side down, in the bottom of the dish. Cover with the lid, reduce the setting to Low, and cook for 2½ hours, until the beef and mushrooms are tender and cooked through. Drain well.

5 To serve, split the burger buns and fill with salad leaves. Pop a mushroom burger into each and serve immediately with extra ketchup to accompany.

COOK'S NOTE

Try the same recipe using pork, chicken or turkey mince.

MACARONI CHEESE WITH HAM, MUSHROOM AND **TOMATO**

Macaroni was just about the only pasta shape on the menu when I was growing up in the 70s. Even though we have a huge choice today, I have to be honest, macaroni cheese is still one of my favourite pasta dishes!

PREPARATION
20 minutes

COOKING TIME
7 minutes
+ 3 hours on Low

SERVES 4

Salt
225 g (8 oz) macaroni
250 g (9 oz) open cup mushrooms
25 g (1 oz) butter
115 g (4 oz) lean ham
3 medium-size ripe tomatoes

50 g (2 oz) freshly grated Parmesan
  cheese
600 ml (1 pt) ready-made cheese sauce
Freshly ground black pepper
Handful of fresh basil, to garnish

1 Put the slow cooker on High to preheat for 20 minutes while you prepare the pasta.

2 Bring a saucepan of lightly salted water to the boil, add the macaroni, bring back to the boil, and cook for 2 minutes. Drain well and set aside.

3 Meanwhile, wipe the mushrooms and slice thickly. Melt the butter in a frying pan until bubbling and hot. Stir-fry the mushrooms for 5 minutes until slightly softened. Set aside. Cut the ham into small pieces. Wash, dry and slice the tomatoes.

4 Put the macaroni into the slow cooker dish and mix in the mushrooms and pan juices, ham and grated cheese. Pour over the cheese sauce and mix gently to make sure the pasta is coated. Arrange the tomato slices on top and season with black pepper. Cover with the lid, reduce the setting to Low, and cook for about 3 hours until tender and piping hot.

5 To serve, spoon on to warm plates and sprinkle with basil leaves. Serve immediately.

COOK'S NOTE

For a less cheesy version, replace the cheese sauce with a tomato-based pasta sauce. For a simple accompaniment, serve with a crisp salad and crusty bread.

ARROZ VERDE CON POLLO

My slow cooker version of 'green rice with chicken'. A perfect meal-in-one, or serve simply with a chopped avocado, fresh coriander and lime salad.

PREPARATION
20 minutes

COOKING TIME
6 minutes
+ 3 hours on High

SERVES 4

4 x 300 g (10½ oz) chicken quarters
Salt and freshly ground black pepper
2 Tbsp vegetable oil
1 medium onion
2 garlic cloves
1 large green pepper
1 green chilli

Juice of 1 lime
150 g (5½ oz) green beans
Small bunch of fresh coriander
50 g (2 oz) pitted green olives
150 g (5½ oz) easy-cook white rice
450 ml (¾ pt) hot chicken stock

1 Put the slow cooker on High to preheat for 20 minutes while you prepare the chicken.

2 Wash and pat dry the chicken. Season all over. Heat the oil in a large frying pan until hot, then cook the chicken for 2 to 3 minutes on each side until lightly golden. Set aside.

3 Peel and chop the onion and garlic. Deseed and chop the pepper and chilli.

4 Place the vegetables in the bottom of the slow cooker dish and arrange the chicken pieces and pan juices on top. Add the lime juice, cover with the lid and cook for 2 hours.

5 Meanwhile, top and tail the green beans and cut into 2.5 cm (1 in) lengths. Roughly chop the coriander and olives. Lift out the chicken using tongs and set aside in a warm dish. Stir the beans, half the coriander, the olives and rice into the cooker dish, pour in the hot stock and then replace the chicken on top. Re-cover and cook for a further hour until the chicken is cooked through (the internal temperature should read 80°C/176°F using a food probe), and the rice is tender with the liquid almost absorbed.

6 To serve, lift out the chicken and remove the skin (and bones if preferred), and place on to warm serving plates. Drain the rice if necessary and pile on to the plates. Sprinkle with the remaining coriander and serve immediately.

MY FAVOURITE **CHICKEN LIVER PÂTÉ**

This classic dish is so easy to put together. It makes a lovely starter or light snack on toasted bread, or something a little different as a sandwich filling.

PREPARATION
20 minutes
+ cooling and chilling

COOKING TIME
5 minutes
+ 3 hours on Low

SERVES 4–6

115 g (4 oz) lean, rindless smoked
   bacon, plus 1 extra rasher
1 garlic clove
1 small onion
25 g (1 oz) butter
225 g (8 oz) chicken livers
Salt and freshly ground black pepper

1 Tbsp freshly chopped thyme
   or 1 tsp dried
2 Tbsp dry sherry or chicken stock
2 Tbsp double cream
1 bay leaf
Salad leaves and crisp toast slices,
   to serve

1 Put the slow cooker on High to preheat for 20 minutes while you prepare the pâté. Lightly grease a 12 cm (5 in) round, ovenproof dish – make sure the dish fits in your slow cooker.

2 Chop 115 g (4 oz) bacon. Peel and chop the garlic and onion. Melt the butter in a frying pan until bubbling and then stir-fry the bacon, garlic and onion for 4 minutes. Add the chicken livers and stir-fry for a further minute. Set aside for 10 minutes.

3 Transfer the liver mixture to a blender or food processor, season well and add the thyme, sherry or stock and cream. Blitz for a few seconds until smooth. Spoon into the prepared dish and smooth the top.

4 Trim the fat from the remaining bacon rasher and cut into four strips. Put the bay leaf on top of the pâté, in the centre, and arrange the bacon strips, two each side of the leaf. Cover the dish with a layer of foil, shiny-side down.

5 Stand the ovenproof dish in the slow cooker dish and pour in sufficient hot water to come halfway up the sides of the pâté dish. Cover with the lid, reduce the setting to Low, and cook for about 3 hours until firm and the juices run clear. Remove from the cooker, peel back the foil and allow to cool. Cover and chill for at least 2 hours.

6 To serve, discard the bay leaf and spoon on to serving plates. Accompany with salad leaves and crisp toast slices.

SWEET PEPPERS WITH SAUSAGE AND FENNEL

If you have a smaller slow cooker, halve the recipe to serve two as a main course or four as a starter.

PREPARATION
20 minutes

COOKING TIME
2½ hours on Low
+ 3 minutes grilling

SERVES 4

2 red peppers
2 yellow peppers
Small bunch of fresh sage
450 g (1 lb) fresh pork sausagemeat
75 g (2½ oz) sultanas
Salt and freshly ground black pepper
2 small bulbs fresh fennel
4 tsp fennel seeds
8 Tbsp freshly grated Parmesan cheese

1 Put the slow cooker on High to preheat for 20 minutes while you prepare the peppers.

2 Cut each pepper in half through the stalk. Carefully scoop out the seeds and inner white membrane, leaving the stalk intact. Reserving a few sage leaves for cooking, finely chop six to eight leaves and place in a small bowl. Mix in the sausagemeat with the sultanas and plenty of seasoning. Divide into eight pieces and set aside.

3 Trim away the wispy fronds from the fennel bulbs and reserve. Slice off the stalks and take off the root end. Cut each bulb into four equal slices lengthways and carefully fit a slice of fennel into each pepper half – you may need to trim the fennel in order to make it fit snuggly. Press the sausagemeat mixture on top.

4 Line the bottom of the slow cooker dish with baking parchment and arrange the peppers, side by side, in the bottom of the dish. Scatter the remaining sage leaves on top. Cover with the lid, reduce the setting to Low, and cook for about 2½ hours until tender and cooked through. Discard the sage leaves.

5 To serve, preheat the grill to a hot setting. Remove the peppers using a draining spoon and arrange in the grill tray. Sprinkle the tops of the peppers lightly with the fennel seeds and then the cheese. Cook under the grill for 2 to 3 minutes until bubbling and golden. Serve immediately garnished with the reserved fennel fronds.

SESAME HOISIN **DRUMSTICKS**

Meat on the bone cooks very tenderly in the slow cooker, and these tasty morsels are no exception. Great picnic or party food served cold with salad – wrap a piece of foil round the ends for easy pick-up.

PREPARATION
20 minutes

COOKING TIME
2 hours on High

SERVES 4

8 medium-size chicken drumsticks
2.5 cm (1 in) piece root ginger
1 garlic clove
2 Tbsp hoisin sauce
1 Tbsp clear honey
2 Tbsp toasted sesame seeds

1 Tbsp sesame oil, optional
2 spring onions, trimmed and finely
    shredded, to garnish
Rice or noodles and stir-fried
    vegetables, to serve

1 Put the slow cooker on High to preheat for 20 minutes while you prepare the chicken.

2 Remove the skin from the drumsticks. Wash and pat dry, then, using a sharp knife, score each piece of chicken in a crisscross design. Place in a shallow dish.

3 Peel and finely chop the ginger and garlic and place in a small bowl. Mix in the hoisin sauce and honey. Brush all over the chicken – for a more intense flavour, cover and chill for 2 hours before cooking.

4 Line the bottom of the cooker dish with baking parchment and arrange the chicken drumsticks, side by side, in the bottom of the dish, spooning over any remaining sauce. Sprinkle with sesame seeds. Cover with the lid, and cook for 2 hours until the chicken is tender and cooked through (the internal temperature should read 80°C/176°F using a food probe). Drain well.

5 If serving hot, arrange on a warm serving platter and drizzle with sesame oil, if using, and spoon over the cooking juices. Garnish with shredded spring onions and serve accompanied with freshly cooked rice or noodles and stir-fried vegetables. To serve cold, drizzle with sesame oil, if using, and allow to cool. Cover and chill for at least 1 hour before serving with a crisp salad.

TARTIFLETTE

A French dish of layered potatoes and bacon cooked in a creamy garlic sauce.
Serve as a simple supper or as a rich vegetable accompaniment.

PREPARATION
25 minutes

COOKING TIME
5 minutes
+ 4 hours on Low

SERVES 4

1 medium onion
2 garlic cloves
8 rashers rindless smoked streaky
  bacon
900 g (2 lb) all-purpose potatoes
300 ml (½ pt) single cream

200 g (7 oz) carton reduced-fat soft
  cheese with herbs and garlic
4 Tbsp freshly chopped chives
15 g (½ oz) butter, softened
Salt and freshly ground black pepper
Crispy salad, to serve

1 Put the slow cooker on High to preheat for 20 minutes while you prepare the tartiflette.

2 Peel and finely chop the onion and garlic, and cut the bacon into small pieces. Place in a frying pan and heat gently, stirring, until the bacon juices run, then dry-fry for 5 minutes.

3 Peel the potatoes, and slice very thinly and evenly. In a bowl, mix together the cream and soft cheese, along with half the chives until well blended.

4 Grease the inside of the slow cooker dish with the butter and layer quarter of the potato in the bottom; season well. Top with some of the onion and bacon mixture, and then continue layering as above until all the ingredients are used up, finishing with a layer of potatoes.

5 Pour over the creamy cheese mixture, allowing it to seep through the layers. Season the top, then cover the top of the dish with a layer of foil, shiny-side down, and then cover with the lid. Reduce the setting to Low and cook for 4 hours until tender.

6 To serve, sprinkle the top with the remaining chives and serve with a crisp salad to accompany.

COOK'S NOTE

Make sure you cut the potatoes evenly and as thinly as possible so that the dish cooks evenly throughout.

FIVE-SPICE **LAMB AND RICE PATTIES** WITH SWEET AND SOUR VEGETABLES

An unusual dish, Chinese-inspired, and very simple to put together. It makes an interesting starter to an Oriental meal.

PREPARATION
20 minutes

COOKING TIME
3 hours on Low

SERVES 4

1 bunch of spring onions
1 red pepper
1 medium carrot
100 g (3½ oz) baby corn
1 garlic clove
350 g (12½ oz) lean minced lamb
100 g (3½ oz) easy-cook white rice
1 Tbsp dark soy sauce
1 tsp Chinese five-spice powder

300 ml (½ pt) hot chicken or vegetable
   stock
2 Tbsp white wine vinegar
2 Tbsp caster sugar
1 Tbsp tomato purée
1 Tbsp cornflour
115 g (4 oz) canned pineapple pieces in
   natural juice, drained
Prawn crackers (optional), to serve

1 Put the slow cooker on High to preheat for 20 minutes while you prepare the vegetables and patties.

2 Trim and chop the spring onions. Deseed and chop the pepper. Peel and finely chop the carrot. Trim and slice the baby corn. Peel and crush the garlic. Put the lamb in a bowl and mix in the garlic, rice, soy sauce and five-spice powder. Mix well together and divide into eight equal portions. Form each into a patty about 1 cm (½ in) thick.

3 Reserving a handful of chopped spring onions for the garnish, put the remaining in the slow cooker dish, along with the pepper, carrot and baby corn, and pour over the hot stock. Arrange the patties, side by side, on top. Cover with the lid, reduce the setting to Low, and cook for 2 hours.

4 Meanwhile, mix together the vinegar, sugar, tomato purée and cornflour to make a smooth paste. Blend with 150 ml (¼ pt) cold water.

5 Remove the patties from the cooker and set aside. Stir the pineapple pieces and tomato stock into the vegetables. Put the patties back on top, the other side down, re-cover and continue to cook for a further hour until cooked through and the vegetables are tender.

6 To serve, remove the patties and place on to warm serving plates. Mix the vegetables together until well mixed and serve with the patties. Garnish with the reserved spring onions. Accompany with prawn crackers, if liked.

HONEY AND MUSTARD **SALMON** WITH BALSAMIC LEMON **COURGETTES**

A light and healthy fish supper. The slow cooker acts as a steamer and captures all the flavours and textures of the ingredients.

PREPARATION
20 minutes

COOKING TIME
1½ hours on High

SERVES 4

4 x 150–200 g (5½–7 oz) thick salmon
    fillets or steaks
Salt and freshly ground black pepper
2 Tbsp wholegrain mustard
1 Tbsp clear honey
2 large courgettes

Finely grated rind of 1 lemon
1 Tbsp balsamic vinegar
1 Tbsp olive oil
Handful of small basil leaves
Lemon wedges
Crushed boiled new potatoes, to serve

1 Put the slow cooker on High to preheat for 20 minutes while you prepare the salmon and courgettes.

2 Wash and pat dry the salmon. Season all over. In a small bowl, mix the mustard and honey together and set aside.

3 Trim the courgettes and then either slice thinly or, using a vegetable peeler, pare the flesh in to ribbon-like strips. Line the bottom of the slow cooker dish with baking parchment and lay the courgettes evenly on top. Season lightly and sprinkle with the lemon rind, vinegar and olive oil.

4 Lay the salmon fillets on top, side by side, and brush the tops with the mustard and honey. Cover with the lid, and cook for about 1½ hours until tender and cooked through.

5 To serve, drain the salmon and courgettes, and serve on warm plates. Sprinkle with fresh basil and accompany with lemon wedges and freshly cooked and crushed potatoes.

COOK'S NOTE

This method of cooking chunky pieces of fish will also work with white fish steaks, whole trout, mackerel and red mullet, and tuna steaks.

SLOW-COOKED **THAI-STYLE MUSSELS** IN A SPICY COCONUT BROTH

The fragrant Thai cooking aromas and flavours of this dish are mouth-watering. Serve with a spoon so you can eat up all the cooking stock as well!

PREPARATION
10 minutes

COOKING TIME
5 minutes
+ 2 hours on Low
+ 50 minutes on High

SERVES 4

1 small onion
2 garlic cloves
1 stalk lemongrass
1 hot red chilli
2 Tbsp vegetable oil
2 tsp coriander seeds, lightly crushed
900 ml (1½ pt) hot fish stock

300 ml (½ pt) reduced-fat coconut milk
2 kaffir lime leaves
Nam pla (fish sauce) or salt, to taste
1 kg (2 lb 3 oz) fresh mussels
Small bunch of fresh coriander
1 lime

1 Peel the onion and garlic and chop very finely. Trim the lemongrass stalk away from the bulb. Peel away the outer leaves and then finely chop the fleshy part of the bulb. Deseed and finely chop the chilli.

2 Heat the oil in a frying pan until hot and fry the onion, garlic, lemongrass, chilli and coriander seeds for 5 minutes until softened but not browned.

3 Transfer to the slow cooker dish and pour in the hot stock and coconut milk. Add the lime leaves and season lightly with the nam pla or salt. Cover with the lid, switch the cooker on to Low and cook for 2 hours to infuse the flavours together, then raise the setting to High and cook for a further 20 minutes.

4 Meanwhile, prepare the mussels. Wash and scrub the mussel shells and remove the hairy 'beards'. Discard any gaping or broken mussels.

5 Add the mussels to the slow cooker dish and stir to mix in the sauce. Cover and cook for about 30 minutes until the shells have opened. Discard any that don't open, along with the lime leaves. Roughly chop the coriander and quarter the lime.

6 To serve, ladle into large, warm shallow bowls and sprinkle with chopped coriander. Accompany with wedges of lime to squeeze over.

BAKED TROUT FILLED WITH MIDDLE EASTERN SPICED ALMOND RICE

Cooked rice makes an excellent stuffing ingredient as it absorbs flavours from other ingredients very well. You can use cooked bulgar wheat or couscous as an alternative.

PREPARATION
20 minutes

COOKING TIME
5 minutes
+ 1 hour on High

SERVES 4

4 whole trout, cleaned
Salt and freshly ground black pepper
1 small red onion
25 g (1 oz) butter
Small bunch of fresh coriander,
    plus extra to garnish
100 g (3½ oz) cooked white
    or brown rice

25 g (1 oz) chopped dried apricots
    or sultanas
½ tsp ground cinnamon
15 g (½ oz) toasted flaked almonds,
    lightly crushed
2 lemons
Steamed vegetables or crisp salad,
    to serve

1 Put the slow cooker on High to preheat for 20 minutes while you prepare the trout.

2 Wash and pat dry the trout and season the cavities. Measure the trout to make sure they will fit side by side in your slow cooker. If necessary, cut off the heads and/or tails. Set aside.

3 Peel and finely chop the onion. Melt the butter in a small frying pan until bubbling, and lightly fry the onion for 5 minutes until softened.

4 Finely chop a few sprigs of the fresh coriander and put in a small bowl. Mix in the rice, apricots or sultanas, cinnamon and almonds. Bind together with the onion and butter mixture and pack neatly into each of the trout cavities.

5 Line the bottom of the cooker dish with baking parchment and arrange the trout, side by side, in the bottom of the dish. Slice one of the lemons and lay a few slices on top of the trout, along with a few more sprigs of coriander. Cover with the lid and cook for about 1 hour until tender and cooked through.

6 To serve, drain the fish using a fish slice and place on to warm serving plates. Serve with the reserved lemon cut into slices, fresh coriander and cooked vegetables or crisp salad.

COOK'S NOTE

This recipe also works well with other types of whole fish, such as small mackerel, mullet or bass.

SUN-DRIED TOMATO, OLIVE AND RED LENTIL **TERRINE**

A recipe in two stages, with no other cooking apart from letting your slow cooker do it all for you. Full of sunny flavours, serve this slice cold as a pâté or as a supper dish, or warm with lots of crisp salad.

PREPARATION
40 minutes + cooling

COOKING TIME
3½ hours on High

SERVES 4

50 g (2 oz) dry-pack pitted black olives
50 g (2 oz) dry-pack sundried tomatoes
1 large carrot
1 small onion
1 stick celery
175 g (6 oz) red lentils

1½ tsp ground cumin
600 ml (1 pt) hot vegetable stock
200 g (7 oz) can chopped tomatoes
2 medium eggs, beaten
Salt and freshly ground black pepper
Salad and toast, to serve

1   Put the slow cooker on High to preheat for 20 minutes while you prepare the terrine.

2   Finely chop the olives and sun-dried tomatoes and place in a bowl. Peel the carrot and grate into the bowl. Cover and chill until required.

3   Peel and finely chop the onion. Trim and finely chop the celery. Put the lentils in a sieve and rinse in cold running water. Shake off the excess water and tip into the slow cooker dish. Stir in the onion, celery and cumin. Pour in the hot stock and chopped tomatoes. Cover with the lid and cook for 1½ hours until the lentils are tender and have absorbed most of the liquid.

4   Switch off the slow cooker. Turn the lentil mixture into a heatproof bowl and allow to cool. When cold, wash and dry the slow cooker dish.

5   When the lentil mixture is cold, reheat the slow cooker as above. Grease and line a 900 g (2 lb) loaf tin – make sure the tin fits in your slow cooker. Mix the prepared olives, sundried tomatoes and carrot into the lentil mixture, along with the eggs and plenty of seasoning. Pile into the prepared loaf tin, and cover the surface with a piece of baking parchment and then cover the tin with a layer of foil.

6   Stand the tin in the slow cooker and carefully pour in sufficient hot water to come halfway up the sides of the tin. Cover with the lid and cook for 2 hours until firm and set. Remove from the slow cooker, unwrap and stand on a wire rack to cool for 30 minutes before turning out of the tin on to a warm serving platter. Serve warm, sliced, with salad. Alternatively, allow to cool completely in the tin. Cover and chill for at least 2 hours before removing from the tin and serving cold as a terrine with toast and salad.

GOLDEN VEGETABLE **RISOTTO**

I use the yellow variety of courgette for this recipe, so you end up with a bright and cheery rice dish guaranteed to gladden the heart. The green ones work just as well though.

PREPARATION
15 minutes

COOKING TIME
8 minutes
+ 2½ hours on Low

SERVES 4

1 small butternut squash or small
   pumpkin
1 large orange or yellow pepper
1 L (1¾ pt) hot vegetable stock
Few sprigs of fresh rosemary,
   plus extra to garnish
1 onion

1 large yellow courgette
25 g (1 oz) butter, melted
300 g (10½ oz) Arborio rice
Salt and freshly ground black pepper
1 large ripe tomato, to garnish
100 g (3½ oz) firm goat's cheese

1 Peel the squash and scoop out the seeds. Cut into pieces about ½ cm (¼ in) thick. Deseed and chop the pepper. Put the vegetables in the slow cooker dish.

2 Pour over 300 ml (½ pt) of the hot stock and add a few sprigs of rosemary. Cover with the lid, switch the cooker on to Low, and cook for 1½ hours, then discard the rosemary.

3 Meanwhile, peel and chop the onion. Trim the courgette and cut into small cubes. Melt the butter in a frying pan until bubbling, and gently fry the onion and courgette for 5 minutes until slightly softened. Add the rice and cook, stirring for 1 minute, until the rice is buttery all over. Pour in a little of the hot stock and simmer gently for 2 minutes until it is absorbed.

4 Transfer the rice mixture to the slow cooker, pour over the remaining stock, season and mix well. Re-cover and continue to cook on Low for a further hour, stirring halfway through, until the rice is tender, thick and creamy.

5 To serve, finely chop the tomato. Pile the risotto into warm, shallow serving bowls. Crumble over the goat's cheese and garnish with chopped tomato and fresh rosemary.

BEEF SAUSAGE, BEETROOT AND POTATO **HASH**

A vibrant supper dish that tastes as good as it looks. Serve with horseradish sauce for extra tang.

PREPARATION
20 minutes

COOKING TIME
9 minutes
+ 5 hours on Low

SERVES 4

500 g (1 lb 2 oz) beetroot
500 g (1 lb 2 oz) general-purpose potatoes
1 large onion
25 g (1 oz) butter
1 tsp caraway seeds
2 bay leaves

Salt and freshly ground black pepper
300 ml (½ pt) hot beef stock
1 Tbsp vegetable oil
8–12 thick beef sausages
4 Tbsp freshly chopped parsley
Horseradish sauce

1 Put the slow cooker on High to preheat for 20 minutes while you prepare the vegetables.

2 Carefully peel the beetroot (see Cook's note) and cut into 5 mm (¼ in) chunks. Set aside. Peel the potatoes and cut in the same way. Peel and chop the onion.

3 Melt the butter in a frying pan until bubbling and gently fry the vegetables for 5 minutes, until just beginning to soften.

4 Pile the vegetable mixture into the slow cooker dish, and mix in the caraway seeds and bay leaves. Season well and pour over the hot stock. Cover the top of the dish with a layer of foil, shiny-side down, and then cover with the lid. Reduce the setting to Low and cook for 2 hours.

5 Just before the end of cooking time, heat the oil in a frying pan until very hot and seal the sausages for 4 minutes until golden brown all over. Carefully remove the lid and foil covering, stir the beetroot and potato mixture, and arrange the sausages on top. Re-cover with the lid only and continue to cook for a further 3 hours, until tender and cooked through. Discard the bay leaves.

6 To serve, drain the vegetables and pile on to warm serving plates. Top with the sausages and sprinkle with chopped parsley. Serve the pot juices as a gravy and accompany with horseradish sauce, if liked.

COOK'S NOTE

Remember, beetroot will stain your fingers, so you may want to wear thin gloves when peeling it.

MOROCCAN SPICED **LAMB SHANKS** WITH APRICOTS

Lamb shanks have become very trendy over the past few years. The meat is very flavoursome and what's more, they are inexpensive to buy.

PREPARATION
20 minutes

COOKING TIME
10 minutes
+ 4½ hours on Low

SERVES 4

150 g (5½ oz) dried apricots
4 x 225 g (8 oz) lean lamb shanks
Salt and freshly ground black pepper
2 tsp cumin seeds, lightly crushed
2 tsp coriander seeds, lightly crushed
2 Tbsp olive oil
1 large onion
1 garlic clove

1 cinnamon stick, broken
400 g (14 oz) can chopped tomatoes
400 g (14 oz) can chickpeas, drained
 and rinsed
600 ml (1 pt) hot chicken or vegetable
 stock
Small bunch of fresh coriander
Rice, couscous or crusty bread, to serve

1 Put the slow cooker on High to preheat for 20 minutes while you prepare the lamb.

2 Cut the apricots into strips; rinse, pat dry and set aside. Wash and pat dry the lamb shanks, trimming away any excess fat. Mix some seasoning together with the cumin and coriander seeds and then rub into the lamb, all over. Heat the oil in a large frying pan until hot and cook the lamb shanks for about 5 minutes, turning in the oil, to seal all over. Transfer to a heatproof plate using tongs, reserving the cooking juices in the pan, and set aside.

3 Peel the onion and garlic and chop finely. Reheat the juices until bubbling and cook the onion and garlic, stirring, for 5 minutes until softened.

4 Arrange the lamb shanks in the slow cooker dish and spoon over the onion, garlic and sliced apricots. Add the cinnamon stick, tomatoes and chickpeas, then pour over the hot stock. Season well, cover with the lid, reduce the setting to Low, and cook for about 4½ hours, until the lamb is falling off the bone. Discard the cinnamon stick.

5 To serve, ladle the lamb on to warm serving plates and sprinkle generously with roughly chopped coriander. Serve with rice, couscous or simply with crusty bread to mop up the juices.

MY GRANNY'S **BEEF STEW** WITH 'DOUGHBOYS'

This type of stew is the perfect opportunity to explore the cheaper cuts of meat like chuck steak, brisket, blade or shin of beef, now making a real comeback. All these cuts cook so tenderly in a slow cooker and have great flavour.

PREPARATION
20 minutes

COOKING TIME
10 minutes
+ 9 hours on Low

SERVES 4

1 large onion
450 g (1 lb) carrots
675 g (1½ lb) stewing beef
3 Tbsp plain flour
Salt and freshly ground black pepper
4 rashers rindless unsmoked streaky
  bacon
25 g (1 oz) dripping or butter

1 Tbsp vegetable oil
750 ml (1¼ pt) hot beef stock
2 bay leaves
175 g (6 oz) self-raising flour,
  plus extra for dusting
75 g (2½ oz) beef suet
Freshly cooked green beans, to serve

1 Peel and chop the onion and carrots. Cut the beef into 2 cm (¾ in) thick pieces and put in a bowl. Toss in the flour and season well. Mix together, making sure the beef is well coated in the flour. Chop the bacon.

2 Melt the dripping or butter with the oil in a large frying pan until bubbling and fry the flour-coated beef, stirring, for about 5 minutes until browned all over. Using a draining spoon, transfer to the slow cooker dish. Reheat the pan juices and gently fry the onion and bacon for 5 minutes until softened, then mix into the beef along with the carrots.

3 Pour over the hot stock and add the bay leaves. Cover with the lid, switch the cooker on to the Low setting, and cook for 8 hours, until the beef is very tender. Discard the bay leaves.

4 Just before the end of cooking time, make the 'doughboys' (dumplings). Sift the flour into a bowl and stir in the suet. Season well and stir in approximately 150 ml (¼ pt) cold water to form a softish dough. Lightly dust your hands and work surface with a little more flour and knead the dough lightly. Form into eight equal portions and shape into balls.

5 Stir the stew well. Arrange the dumplings around the edge of the slow cooker dish, re-cover and continue to cook for a further hour until the dumplings are risen and cooked through.

6 To serve, ladle the stew and dumplings on to warm serving plates, and accompany with freshly cooked green beans.

A PROPER **BEEF CHILLI**

Made with chunks of beef rather than beef mince, this is another recipe where cheap stewing cuts (see page 69) can be used with great results.

PREPARATION
20 minutes

COOKING TIME
20 minutes
+ 10 hours on Low

SERVES 4

150 g (5½ oz) dried kidney beans, soaked overnight
675 g (1½ lb) stewing beef
1 Tbsp malt vinegar
1 tsp caster sugar
2 tsp dried chilli flakes, plus extra to serve
2 tsp ground cumin
Salt and freshly ground black pepper
1 large onion

2 garlic cloves
3 Tbsp vegetable oil
1 small cinnamon stick
4 Tbsp tomato purée
2 Tbsp plain flour
500 ml (18 fl oz) hot beef stock
400 g (14 oz) can chopped tomatoes
Small bunch of fresh coriander
Soured cream and tortilla chips, to serve

1 Rinse and drain the kidney beans. Put in a saucepan, cover with water and bring to the boil. Boil rapidly for 10 minutes (see page 10), then drain well and set aside.

2 Meanwhile, cut the beef into 2 cm (¾ in) thick cubes and put in a bowl. Mix in the vinegar, sugar, 2 teaspoons of chilli, cumin and plenty of seasoning. Set aside while preparing the vegetables.

3 Peel and chop the onion and garlic. Heat the oil in a large frying pan and gently fry the vegetables for 5 minutes until just softened. Using a draining spoon, transfer to the slow cooker dish and add the cinnamon stick, beans and tomato purée. Mix well.

4 Mix the flour into the beef. Reheat the frying pan juices until hot and then stir-fry the flour-coated beef for 5 minutes until sealed all over. Transfer the pan contents to the slow cooker dish and mix well.

5 Pour over the hot stock and mix in the tomatoes. Cover with the lid, switch the cooker on to Low, and cook for about 10 hours, until the meat and beans are tender. Discard the cinnamon stick.

6 To serve, spoon into warm serving bowls and serve with fresh coriander, soured cream and tortilla chips. Accompany with a crisp salad and sprinkle with chilli flakes if liked.

PESTO **TURKEY MEATBALLS** IN RED PEPPER AND OLIVE SAUCE

Super lean turkey mince makes a tasty and lower-fat alternative to traditional beef in this recipe.

PREPARATION
20 minutes

COOKING TIME
10 minutes
+ 2 hours on High

SERVES 4

500 g (1 lb 2 oz) turkey mince
2 Tbsp grated Parmesan cheese
75 g (2½ oz) fresh white breadcrumbs
Salt and freshly ground black pepper
2 Tbsp green pesto sauce
2 Tbsp olive oil
1 onion
1 garlic clove
1 large red pepper

400 g (14 oz) can chopped tomatoes
150 ml (¼ pt) dry white wine
1 bay leaf
1 tsp dried oregano
2 tsp caster sugar
75 g (2½ oz) pitted black olives, halved
Freshly cooked tagliatelle, to serve
Fresh basil, to garnish

1 Put the slow cooker on High to preheat for 20 minutes while you prepare the meatballs.

2 In a mixing bowl, mix together the turkey, Parmesan and breadcrumbs. Season well and bind together with the pesto sauce. Divide into 16 portions and roll into balls. Heat the oil in a frying pan until hot and cook the meatballs for about 5 minutes, stirring, until browned all over. Remove from the pan using a slotted spoon.

3 Peel and finely chop the onion and garlic. Deseed and chop the pepper into small chunks. Reheat the pan juices and gently fry the onion, garlic and pepper for 5 minutes, until softened. Stir in the tomatoes, wine, bay leaf, oregano, sugar and seasoning, then transfer to the slow cooker dish.

4 Arrange the meatballs on top, cover with the lid, and cook for 2 hours until the meatballs are cooked through. Remove the meatballs using a slotted spoon and keep warm. Discard the bay leaf and blitz the sauce using a hand blender for a few seconds until smooth. Stir in the olives.

5 To serve, spoon the sauce over freshly cooked tagliatelle and top with the meatballs. Garnish with basil.

POT ROAST **TURKEY DRUMMER**

The leg of the turkey has a slightly gamey flavour and makes a great any-day roast for at least two people. If you have a large slow cooker, you should be able to fit two drumsticks next to each other if you need to feed more.

PREPARATION
20 minutes

COOKING TIME
9 minutes
+ 2 hours on High

SERVES 2–3

1 large onion
1 large carrot
1 large parsnip
1 medium turnip
700 g (1 lb 9 oz) turkey drumstick
Salt and freshly ground black pepper

6 rashers rindless smoked streaky bacon
2 Tbsp vegetable oil
Few sprigs of fresh thyme
Few sprigs of fresh sage
Freshly cooked green vegetables, to serve

1 Put the slow cooker on High to preheat for 20 minutes while you prepare the pot roast.

2 Peel and chop the onion. Peel the carrot, parsnip and turnip, and cut into small pieces. Set aside.

3 Remove the skin from the turkey, wash and pat dry, then season all over. Wrap the bacon, overlapping, round the turkey and secure in place with pieces of clean string tied at intervals down the length of the drumstick.

4 Heat the oil in a large frying pan until hot and then fry the turkey for 2 minutes, turn over, and cook for a further 2 minutes to brown on both sides. Remove from the pan, reserving the juices, and set aside.

5 Reheat the pan juices and cook the vegetables, stirring, for 5 minutes, until well coated in the juices. Transfer to the slow cooker dish, sprinkle with a few sprigs of thyme and sage, and sit the turkey drumstick on top.

6 Cover with the lid and cook for about 2 hours until tender and cooked through (the internal temperature should read 80°C/176°F using a food probe). Discard the herbs.

7 To serve, drain the turkey and discard the string. Carve or cut into bite-size pieces. Drain the chopped vegetables and serve alongside the turkey, accompanied with the cooking juices if liked and freshly cooked green vegetables.

DEVILLED **POUSSINS**

Poussins have very soft flesh with a slightly sweet flavour. The slow cooker helps retain their succulence. Quarter a small 1 kg (2 lb 3½ oz) chicken if unavailable or use other prepared chicken portions.

PREPARATION
20 minutes

COOKING TIME
5 minutes
+ 2 hours on High

SERVES 4

2 tsp mustard powder
2 tsp smoked or plain paprika
2 tsp ground turmeric
2 tsp ground cumin
4 Tbsp tomato ketchup
2 Tbsp lemon juice
4 Tbsp vegetable oil
2 x 450 g (1 lb) oven-ready poussins

Salt and freshly ground black pepper
2 red onions
2 garlic cloves
1 large red pepper
1 large yellow pepper
1 hot red chilli
2 Tbsp freshly chopped parsley
Steamed rice and salad, to serve

1 Put the slow cooker on High to preheat for 20 minutes while you prepare the poussins.

2 Put all the spices in a small bowl and mix in the ketchup, lemon juice and 2 tablespoons of the oil to make a thick paste. Set aside.

3 Using a large sharp knife, cut each poussin in half along the breastbone through to the backbone. Remove the skin. Wash and pat dry, then season all over. Place in a shallow dish and thickly brush the spice paste over the top of each piece. Set aside.

4 Peel the onions and garlic, and slice thinly. Deseed the peppers and slice thinly. Deseed and finely chop the chilli. Heat the remaining oil in a large frying pan until hot, then stir-fry the vegetables for 5 minutes until softened. Transfer to the slow cooker dish.

5 Carefully arrange the poussin pieces on top of the vegetables, cover with the lid, and cook on High for about 2 hours, until the meat is tender and cooked through (the internal temperature should read 80°C/176°F using a food probe).

6 To serve, drain the poussin and vegetables, and spoon on to warm plates. Serve sprinkled with parsley, and accompanied with steamed rice and a crisp salad.

HONEYED **PORK SAUSAGES** WITH ROOT VEG WEDGES

A contemporary version of sausage and chips. You can add turnip and carrots to the mix as well if liked.

PREPARATION
10 minutes

COOKING TIME
17 minutes
+ 4 hours on Low

SERVES 4

1 large parsnip
1 medium sweet potato
1 large baking potato
3 Tbsp vegetable oil
1 tsp coriander seeds, crushed
Salt and freshly ground black pepper

8–12 thick pork sausages
1 large onion
1 Tbsp freshly chopped sage or
 1 tsp dried sage
1 Tbsp clear honey
2 Tbsp freshly shredded sage leaves

1 Peel the parsnip and sweet potato. Scrub the baking potato. Cut each vegetable into similar-size wedges, approximately 1 cm (½ in) thick. Heat 2 tablespoons of the oil in a large frying pan until hot and then stir-fry the vegetables for 6 to 7 minutes, until lightly browned all over.

2 Transfer the vegetables to the slow cooker dish. Sprinkle with coriander seeds and season well.

3 Heat the remaining oil in the same frying pan until hot and fry the sausages for 4 minutes until golden brown all over. Using tongs, place on top of the root vegetables.

4 Peel the onion and slice thinly. Fry with the sage in the same pan for 5 minutes, stirring, then add the honey and cook for 1 more minute until richly golden. Spoon over the sausages. Cover with the lid and switch the cooker on to Low. Leave to cook for about 4 hours until tender and cooked through.

5 To serve, drain the vegetables and sausages, and serve on warm plates, sprinkled with freshly shredded sage leaves.

COOK'S NOTE

For a more traditional sausage supper, use three baking potatoes instead of the parsnip and sweet potato. Try sprinkling the potatoes with a pinch of chilli powder for an added spicy kick.

HEARTY SMOKED SAUSAGE, CABBAGE AND LENTIL **HOT POT**

Green lentils make this a more substantial supper dish and help make a little meat go a long way.

PREPARATION
25 minutes

COOKING TIME
10 minutes
+ 30 minutes on High
+ 3 hours on Low

SERVES 4

175 g (6 oz) green lentils
1 onion
1 garlic clove
2 sticks celery
1 tsp ground cumin
1 tsp dried chilli flakes,
    plus extra to serve

Salt and freshly ground black pepper
900 ml (1½ pt) hot chicken stock
225 g (8 oz) green cabbage
225 g (8 oz) cooked smoked pork sausage
4 thick slices of toasted French stick,
    to serve

1 Put the slow cooker on High to preheat for 20 minutes while you prepare the lentils.

2 Rinse the lentils in a sieve, then put in a saucepan. Cover with water, bring to the boil and cook for 10 minutes. Drain well and set aside. Peel the onion and garlic and chop finely. Trim and finely chop the celery.

3 Tip the lentils into the slow cooker dish and mix in the vegetables, along with the cumin, chilli and plenty of seasoning. Pour over the hot stock. Cover with the lid and cook for 30 minutes. Reduce the setting to Low and cook for a further 2 hours.

4 Meanwhile, remove any coarse stems from the cabbage and shred the leaves finely. Slice the sausage into 1 cm (½ in) thick pieces. Stir into the lentils, cover and cook for a further hour until tender.

5 To serve, place a slice of toasted French bread in the bottom of four warm shallow soup bowls and ladle over the lentil and sausage mixture. Sprinkle with extra chilli flakes if liked and serve immediately.

COOK'S NOTE

Transform this combination of ingredients into an autumnal feast by using red cabbage instead of green. Replace the spices with six crushed juniper berries, and use roughly chopped chunks of cooked venison sausage instead of the smoked pork. Add a handful of sultanas to help counteract the richness.

CARIBBEAN-STYLE PORK, **RICE 'N' PEAS**

A mixture of lots of Caribbean flavours in one dish. Add the cayenne pepper to taste – remember it is quite spicy hot! Omit the pork and it makes a delicious side dish to go with grilled or barbecued meat or fish.

PREPARATION
20 minutes + standing

COOKING TIME
15 minutes
+ 2 hours on Low

SERVES 4

150 g (5½ oz) dried black eye beans, soaked overnight
500 g (1 lb 2 oz) lean pork
Salt and freshly ground black pepper
1 Tbsp freshly chopped or
   1 tsp dried thyme
½ to 1 tsp cayenne pepper
1 medium onion
2 garlic cloves

2 Tbsp vegetable oil
225 g (8 oz) easy-cook white rice
50 g (2 oz) creamed coconut
1 small cinnamon stick
900 ml (1½ pt) hot chicken or
   vegetable stock
225 g (8 oz) fresh or canned cubed
   pineapple (optional)
Crisp salad, to serve

1 Put the slow cooker on High to preheat for 20 minutes while you prepare the pork and rice.

2 Rinse and drain the beans. Put in a saucepan, cover with water and bring to the boil. Boil rapidly for 10 minutes (see page 10). Drain well and set aside.

3 Wash and pat dry the pork, then cut into pieces about 2 cm (¾ in) thick. Place in a bowl and mix in plenty of seasoning, along with the thyme and cayenne pepper, to taste. Set aside.

4 Peel and chop the onion and garlic. Heat the oil in a large frying pan until hot, then fry the pork with the onion and garlic for 5 minutes, stirring, until browned all over.

5 Transfer the pork mixture to the slow cooker dish. Mix in the rice and beans. Add the creamed coconut and cinnamon stick, and pour over the hot stock. Cover with the lid, reduce the setting to Low, and cook for 2 hours until the pork, rice and beans are tender and the liquid has just about absorbed. Switch off the cooker, remove the dish and stand on a heatproof surface. Stir in the pineapple, if using, and leave, covered for a further 20 minutes. Discard the cinnamon stick.

6 Serve immediately, spooned on to warm serving plates and accompany with a crisp salad.

THAI GREEN PORK AND VEGETABLE **CURRY**

It's worth taking a trip to an Oriental supermarket to buy the ingredients for this dish – in this instance, fresh is definitely best. This popular Thai dish combines the heat of chilli with the fragrance of galangal and lemongrass.

PREPARATION
25 minutes

COOKING TIME
6 minutes
+ 2 hours on Low

SERVES 4

2 lemongrass stalks
2.5 cm (1 in) piece galangal or root ginger
2 shallots
2 garlic cloves
1 small red chilli
1 tsp coriander seeds, crushed
2 Tbsp nam pla (fish sauce)
500 g (1 lb 2 oz) lean pork
2 Tbsp vegetable oil

300 ml (½ pt) canned coconut milk
600 ml (1 pt) hot chicken stock
150 g (5½ oz) baby corn
150 g (5½ oz) sugar snap peas
1 bunch of spring onions
Small bunch of fresh coriander,
   plus extra to garnish
Steamed jasmine rice, to serve

1 Put the slow cooker on High to preheat for 20 minutes while you prepare the curry.

2 Trim the base off each stalk of lemongrass. Slice off the bulb and discard the outer leaves. Finely chop the bulb. Peel and finely chop the galangal or ginger, shallots and garlic. Deseed and finely chop the chilli. Place all the ingredients in a small bowl and mix in the coriander seeds and fish sauce to make a chunky paste.

3 Wash and pat dry the pork. Cut into pieces about 2 cm (¾ in) thick. Heat the oil in a frying pan until hot and stir-fry the spice paste for 1 minute, then add the pork. Continue to stir-fry for a further 5 minutes, until browned all over.

4 Transfer all the ingredients to the slow cooker dish and pour over the coconut milk and hot stock. Cover with the lid, reduce the setting to Low, and cook for 1 hour.

5 Meanwhile, prepare the vegetables. Trim and halve the baby corn. Trim the sugar snap peas and slice in half diagonally. Trim and chop the spring onions and the fresh coriander. Stir the vegetables into the pork, re-cover, and cook for a further hour until the pork and vegetables are tender.

6 To serve, ladle the curry over freshly cooked jasmine rice and garnish with more fresh coriander.

PLAICE AND SMOKED SALMON **ROLLS** WITH GOLDEN VEGETABLES

A very pretty dish with delicate shades of yellow and orange. Change the vegetables to suit, but make sure you choose vegetables that cook in the same way.

PREPARATION 30 minutes	1 medium onion
	½ small butternut squash
COOKING TIME 5 minutes + 1½ hours on Low + 1 hour 20 minutes on High	1 large yellow courgette
	1 yellow or orange pepper
	150 g (5½ oz) baby corn
	50 g (2 oz) butter
SERVES 4	1 bay leaf
	150 ml (¼ pt) dry white wine

150 ml (¼ pt) hot fish stock
4 x 150 g (5½ oz) skinless plaice fillets
Salt and freshly ground black pepper
4 thin slices smoked salmon, about the same size as the plaice fillets
100 g (3½ oz) reduced-fat soft cheese with garlic and herbs
4 Tbsp freshly chopped dill

1 Peel the onion and chop finely. Scoop out the seeds from the squash and slice off the skin. Cut the flesh into small pieces about ½ cm (¼ in) thick. Trim the courgette, cut in half lengthways and then cut into small pieces.

2 Deseed and chop the pepper into small cubes. Trim the baby corn. Melt the butter in a large frying pan until bubbling, then stir-fry all the vegetables for 5 minutes.

3 Transfer the vegetables and pan juices to the slow cooker dish. Add the bay leaf and pour over the wine and hot stock. Cover with the lid and switch the cooker on to Low. Leave to cook for 1½ hours, until beginning to soften, then raise the setting to High and allow to heat up for 20 minutes.

4 Meanwhile, wash and pat dry the plaice fillets. Season on one side and top with a slice of smoked salmon, trimming to fit neatly as necessary. Carefully spread with the soft cheese and sprinkle with half the dill. Roll up tightly like a Swiss roll and secure the seam with a cocktail stick. Cover and chill until ready to cook.

5 Arrange the plaice fillets on top of the vegetables, seam-side down. Re-cover and continue to cook for about 1 hour on High, until the fish flakes easily. Discard the bay leaf.

6 To serve, drain the vegetables and fish, and spoon on to warm serving plates. Remove the cocktail sticks and sprinkle with the remaining dill.

GARLICKY SMOKED FISH PIE

Finishing off a slow cooker dish with a crisp topping gives a different twist to serving this recipe. Alternatively, try mixing the fish sauce into freshly cooked pasta. Use unsmoked fish if preferred.

PREPARATION
25 minutes

COOKING TIME
3 minutes
+ 1 hour on High

SERVES 4

600 g (1 lb 5 oz) skinless chunky smoked haddock fillet
175 g (6 oz) frozen sweetcorn kernels
175 g (6 oz) frozen peas
1 bunch of spring onions
2 garlic cloves
2 x 400 g (14 oz) cans chopped tomatoes
2 tsp caster sugar

1 bay leaf
Salt and freshly ground black pepper
1 small French stick
100 g (3½ oz) reduced-fat soft cheese with garlic and herbs
75 g (2½ oz) grated mature Cheddar cheese
1 Tbsp freshly chopped parsley

1 Put the slow cooker on High to preheat for 20 minutes while you prepare the fish.

2 Wash and pat dry the fish, and cut into 2.5 cm (1 in) thick pieces. Place in the slow cooker dish, and top with the frozen sweetcorn and peas.

3 Trim and finely chop the spring onions. Peel and crush the garlic. Mix into the chopped tomatoes, along with the sugar. Spoon over the fish and vegetables. Add the bay leaf and season well.

4 Cover with the lid and cook for about 1 hour, until the fish flakes easily. Discard the bay leaf.

5 Just before the end of cooking time, preheat the grill to its hottest setting. Cut the bread into 1 cm (½ in) thick slices and arrange on the grill rack. Cook for about 1 minute on each side until lightly toasted. Spread each slice with soft cheese and press a little grated cheese on top. Replace under the grill for about 1 minute until the cheese melts and bubbles.

6 To serve, arrange the cheesy bread slices around the top of the slow cooker dish, pressing them lightly into the fish sauce. Serve straight from the pot, sprinkled with chopped parsley.

BARBECUE **BAKED BEANS** AND **HAM**

My version of my favourite canned convenience food. There's a smoky-sweet, barbecue note to these beans and the chilli adds a bit of a kick!

PREPARATION
10 minutes
+ overnight soaking

COOKING TIME
10 minutes
+ 8 hours on Low

SERVES 4

350 g (12½ oz) dried haricot beans,
   soaked overnight
900 g (2 lb) smoked ham hock, knuckle
   or shank, soaked overnight
1 medium onion
2 bay leaves
2 tsp smoked paprika
2 Tbsp light brown sugar
2 Tbsp treacle

2 tsp dry mustard powder
1 tsp dried chilli flakes
150 ml (¼ pt) tomato ketchup
900 ml (1½ pt) hot chicken stock
Salt and freshly ground black pepper
2 Tbsp freshly chopped parsley
Toasted crusty bread and tomatoes,
   to serve

1 Rinse and drain the beans. Put in a saucepan, cover with water and bring to the boil. Boil rapidly for 10 minutes (see page 10). Drain well and put in the slow cooker dish. Drain and rinse the ham and push into the centre of the beans.

2 Peel the onion and cut into quarters, then push into the beans along with the bay leaves. In a small bowl, mix together the paprika, sugar, treacle, mustard powder, chilli flakes and ketchup, and then mix into the hot stock. Season lightly.

3 Pour over the beans and ham. Cover the dish with the lid, switch the cooker on to Low and cook for about 8 hours until very tender. Discard the bay leaves and onion.

4 To serve, remove the ham from the beans and take off the ham skin. Shred the ham meat and add it to the beans. Mix well and then spoon on to warm serving plates. Sprinkle with chopped parsley, and serve with toasted crusty bread and sliced tomatoes.

COOK'S NOTE

For a vegetarian version, omit the ham and increase the bean quantity to 450 g (1 lb). Use hot vegetable stock and add a couple of peeled garlic cloves to the mix for extra savouriness. You could try this dish as a hearty breakfast: simply leave to cook overnight for a maximum of 10 hours.

A SORT OF **MOUSSAKA**

I don't think you can shortcut aubergine preparation unless you want to sacrifice the melt-in-the-mouth texture of the finished dish.

PREPARATION
30 minutes + standing

COOKING TIME
11 minutes
+ 3½ hours on High

SERVES 4

550 g (1 lb 3 oz) aubergines
4 Tbsp salt
1 onion
2 garlic cloves
1 Tbsp olive oil
450 g (1 lb) lean minced lamb
1 tsp ground cinnamon
1 tsp dried oregano

400 g (14 oz) can chopped tomatoes
50 g (2 oz) butter
50 g (2 oz) plain flour
600 ml (1 pt) whole milk
Salt and freshly ground black pepper
8 Tbsp freshly grated Parmesan cheese
3 ripe tomatoes
1 medium egg yolk

1 Trim the aubergines and cut into small pieces. Layer in a colander over a bowl, sprinkling with the salt as you go. Stand for 20 minutes. Put the slow cooker on High to preheat for 20 minutes while you prepare the lamb.

2 Peel and chop the onion and garlic. Heat the oil in a frying pan until hot, and stir-fry the onion, garlic, lamb, cinnamon and oregano together for 5 minutes until browned all over. Add the tomatoes, bring to the boil, then remove from the heat and set aside.

3 Thoroughly rinse the aubergines, pat dry and put in the slow cooker dish. Stir in the lamb sauce, cover with the lid and cook for 2½ hours until tender.

4 Meanwhile, melt the butter in a saucepan and blend in the flour. Remove from the heat and gradually stir in the milk. Return to the heat and cook, stirring, until the sauce comes to the boil and thickens. Remove from the heat, season and stir in half the cheese. Set aside.

5 After the 2½ hours' cooking time, thinly slice the tomatoes. Mix the egg yolk into the sauce. Arrange the tomato slices over the lamb and spread the sauce on top. Cover and cook for a further hour until bubbling. Switch off the cooker, remove the dish, and stand uncovered on a wire rack for 15 minutes to set.

6 Preheat the grill to its highest setting. Spread out the remaining cheese in four equal rounds on foil and cook for about 1 minute until melted and golden. Cool until firm, then gently peel from the foil. Serve each portion of moussaka with a Parmesan crisp on top.

CORNBREAD-TOPPED RED PEPPER AND BUTTERBEAN **STEW**

The yellow cornbread batter sets on top of a very tasty bright red bean mixture to make a golden, spongy topping.

PREPARATION
10 minutes

COOKING TIME
15 minutes
+ 5 hours on Low

SERVES 4

350 g (12½ oz) dried butter beans, soaked overnight
1 large onion
1 garlic clove
2 large red peppers
3 Tbsp vegetable oil
2 x 400 g (14 oz) cans chopped tomatoes
2 tsp caster sugar
2 tsp smoked paprika
Salt and freshly ground black pepper

300 ml (½ pt) hot vegetable stock
125 g (4½ oz) cornmeal
1 Tbsp plain flour
2 tsp baking powder
6 Tbsp freshly grated Parmesan cheese
1 medium egg, beaten
150 ml (¼ pt) whole milk
Parsley, to garnish
Crisp salad, to serve

1 Rinse and drain the beans. Put in a saucepan, cover with water and bring to the boil. Boil rapidly for 10 minutes (see page 10). Drain well and set aside.

2 Peel and chop the onion and garlic. Deseed and chop the peppers. Heat 2 tablespoons of the oil in a frying pan until hot and stir-fry the vegetables for 5 minutes until softened.

3 Put the beans in the slow cooker dish and mix in the fried vegetables, along with the tomatoes, sugar, paprika and plenty of seasoning. Pour over the hot stock. Cover the top of the dish with a layer of foil, shiny-side down, and then cover with the lid. Switch the cooker on to Low and cook for 4 hours until tender.

4 Just before the end of cooking time, put the cornmeal in a bowl and mix in the flour, baking powder, cheese and a little seasoning. Make a well in the centre and add the remaining oil, egg and milk, and beat well to form a smooth, thick batter.

5 Carefully remove the lid and foil covering. Spoon the batter roughly over the top of the bean mixture. Re-cover with the lid only and continue to cook for a further hour until the cornbread is firm.

6 To serve, spoon the stew on to warm serving plates, garnish with parsley and serve with a crisp salad.

A REALLY GOOD **VEGETABLE CURRY**

Creamy coconut and a delicate blend of Indian spices help create a curry that the whole family will enjoy. Use any combination of root vegetables, just make sure you cut them to the same thickness for even cooking.

PREPARATION
20 minutes

COOKING TIME
9 minutes
+ 3 hours on High

SERVES 4

6 cardamom pods
1 tsp coriander seeds
1 tsp mustard seeds
2.5 cm (1 in) piece root ginger
2 garlic cloves
3 Tbsp vegetable oil
1 tsp ground turmeric
1 tsp ground cumin

900 g (2 lb) combination of sweet
    potatoes, parsnips, carrots and turnips
600 ml (1 pt) coconut milk
1 tsp salt
225 g (8 oz) small cauliflower florets
4 Tbsp freshly chopped coriander
Freshly cooked Basmati rice or warm
    naan bread, to serve

1 Put the slow cooker on High to preheat for 20 minutes while you prepare the curry.

2 Prize off the green casings from the cardamom pods and place the seeds in a pestle and mortar, along with the coriander and mustard seeds. Crush lightly. Place in a small frying pan and dry-fry the seeds, stirring, for 3 to 4 minutes, until lightly toasted and fragrant. Set aside.

3 Peel and chop the ginger and garlic, and place in a blender or food processor with 1 tablespoon of the oil. Add the toasted spices, turmeric and ground cumin, and blend for a few seconds to make a paste.

4 Peel all the root vegetables and cut into 1 cm (½ in) thick pieces. Heat the remaining oil in a large frying pan and gently fry the spice paste for 3 minutes, until softened but not browned. Add the root vegetables and cook, stirring, for 2 minutes, until well coated in the paste.

5 Transfer the vegetable mixture to the slow cooker dish. Pour over the coconut milk and add the salt. Cover with the lid and cook for about 2½ hours, until just tender. Stir in the cauliflower florets, cover and continue to cook for a further 30 minutes, until all the vegetables are completely tender.

6 Stir in the chopped coriander and serve ladled over freshly cooked rice or with warm naan bread to mop up the sauce.

RATATOUILLE **VEGETABLE LASAGNE**

There are a few shortcuts included in this recipe to make life a bit easier,
but you can make your own sauces if you prefer.

PREPARATION
25 minutes

COOKING TIME
7 minutes
+ 2 hours on Low

SERVES 4

1 aubergine
2 Tbsp salt
1 large onion
2 garlic cloves
2 yellow peppers
1 large courgette
4 Tbsp olive oil
500 g (1 lb 2 oz) carton passata

2 tsp dried oregano
2 tsp caster sugar
Freshly ground black pepper
5–6 no-need-to-precook lasagne sheets
600 ml (1 pt) ready-made cheese sauce
4 Tbsp freshly grated Parmesan cheese
Crisp salad, to serve

1 Trim the aubergine and cut into small pieces about 1 cm (½ in) thick. Layer in a colander or large sieve, sprinkling with the salt as you go. Put the colander in a large bowl and set aside for 20 minutes, then rinse the aubergine well and pat dry with kitchen paper. Meanwhile, put the slow cooker on High to preheat for 20 minutes while you prepare the rest of the dish.

2 Peel and finely chop the onion and garlic. Deseed and finely chop the peppers. Trim and finely chop the courgette.

3 Heat the oil in a large frying pan and gently fry the onion, garlic and peppers for about 5 minutes until softened. Stir in the courgette and aubergine, and cook for 2 minutes. Remove from the heat and stir in the passata, oregano, sugar and plenty of seasoning.

4 Put half the vegetable mixture in the slow cooker dish. Lay sufficient lasagne sheets on top, trimming to fit. Spoon over the remaining vegetables and top with more lasagne sheets. Spoon over the cheese sauce, cover with the lid, reduce the setting to Low, and cook for 2 hours until tender.

5 Just before the end of cooking time, preheat the grill to its highest setting. Spread out the cheese in four equal rounds on foil and cook for about 1 minute until melted and golden. Cool until firm, then gently peel from the foil.

6 To serve, slice and spoon the lasagne on to warm serving dishes and top each portion with a Parmesan crisp. Accompany with a crisp salad.

SMOKY CHICKEN **BAKE**

A dish with a late summer/autumnal feel and a deliciously moreish flavour.
Works well with pheasant or duck portions but remove the skin before cooking.

PREPARATION
20 minutes

COOKING TIME
10 minutes
+ 1 hour on High
+ 6 hours on Low

SERVES 4

1 large onion
2 garlic cloves
1 large red pepper
8 rashers rindless smoked streaky
  bacon
4 chicken legs or quarters
Salt and freshly ground black pepper
2 Tbsp cold pressed rapeseed oil,
  or other vegetable oil

2 bay leaves
1 sprig fresh sage or 1 tsp dried
2 tsp caster sugar
1 tsp smoked paprika
2 x 400 g (14 oz) cans chopped tomatoes
300 ml (½ pt) hot chicken stock
2 Tbsp freshly chopped parsley
Crusty bread and steamed vegetables,
  to serve

1 Put the slow cooker on High to preheat for 20 minutes while you prepare the vegetables and chicken.

2 Peel and chop the onion and garlic. Deseed and chop the pepper. Chop the bacon. Wash and pat dry the chicken and season all over. Heat the oil in a large frying pan until hot, and brown the chicken with the bacon for 5 minutes, turning, until lightly golden. Drain the chicken, reserving the pan juices, and set aside.

3 Reheat the pan juices and cook the onion, garlic and pepper, stirring, for 5 minutes. Transfer the pan contents to the slow cooker dish. Add the herbs, sugar, paprika and tomatoes, and mix well.

4 Arrange the chicken pieces on top, pour over the hot stock and cover with the lid. Cook for 1 hour. Reduce the setting to Low and continue to cook for about 6 hours, until the chicken is tender and falling off the bones. Discard the herbs.

5 To serve, spoon on to warm serving plates, sprinkle with chopped parsley, and accompany with crusty bread and steamed vegetables.

LIGHTLY SPICED INDIAN-STYLE **PILAF**

There's a bit of preparation involved with this dish, but once it's in the slow cooker all you have to do is sit back and wait.

PREPARATION
20 minutes

COOKING TIME
12 minutes
+ 1 hour 15 minutes
on High

SERVES 4

300 g (10½ oz) easy-cook basmati rice
1 large onion
1 mild green chilli
2 tsp each of mustard seeds, cumin
  seeds and coriander seeds
6 cardamom pods
50 g (2 oz) butter
3 Tbsp *methi* (dried fenugreek leaves)
  (see Cook's note)

1 tsp salt
200 g (7 oz) frozen peas
100 g (3½ oz) unsalted cashew nuts
4 Tbsp freshly chopped coriander
Tomato, red onion and cucumber salad,
  to serve

1 Put the slow cooker on High to preheat for 20 minutes while you prepare the rice.

2 Put the rice in a sieve and rinse under cold running water. Drain well and set aside.

3 Peel and finely chop the onion. Deseed and finely chop the chilli. Put the mustard, cumin and coriander seeds in a frying pan and dry-fry for 2 to 3 minutes to 'toast' until slightly golden. Remove from the heat and grind using a pestle and mortar. Add the cardamom pods and crush lightly to split the casings.

4 Melt the butter in a frying pan until bubbling hot, and stir-fry the onions and chilli with the spices for 5 minutes until lightly golden. Remove from the heat and stir in the *methi* and salt.

5 Put the rice in the slow cooker dish and stir in the spiced onion mixture. Pour over 600 ml (1 pt) hot water, cover with the lid and cook for 45 minutes. Stir in the frozen peas, re-cover and cook for a further 30 minutes until tender. Meanwhile, put the cashew nuts in a frying pan and 'toast' as above for 3 to 4 minutes until lightly golden. Set aside.

6 To serve, fork the mixture through, adding the chopped coriander until well mixed. Discard the cardamom pods and spoon on to warm serving plates. Sprinkle with the cashew nuts and serve with a tomato, red onion and cucumber salad.

COOK'S NOTE

This recipe calls for *methi*, or dried fenugreek leaves. The fragrance is typically of curry powder. If unavailable, use 2 teaspoons of a mild curry powder instead.

BEEF **STIFADHO**

A Greek-Cypriot dish of meat cooked in a richly fragrant tomato and wine sauce with garlic, bay, cinnamon and cloves. Delicious.

PREPARATION
15 minutes

COOKING TIME
10 minutes
+ 10 hours on Low

SERVES 4

350 g (12½ oz) baby onions
4 cloves
4 garlic cloves
2 Tbsp vegetable oil
675 g (1½ lb) stewing beef, cut into
   2 cm (¾ in) thick pieces
2 bay leaves
½ tsp freshly ground black pepper
1 small stick cinnamon, broken

4 Tbsp balsamic vinegar
1 Tbsp caster sugar
4 Tbsp tomato purée
2 x 400 g (14 oz) cans chopped tomatoes
1 tsp salt
150 ml (¼ pt) red wine
Freshly cooked rice or hot cracked wheat
   and Greek salad, to serve
2 Tbsp freshly chopped parsley

1 Peel the baby onions and leave whole. Stud one of the onions with the cloves. Peel and finely chop the garlic.

2 Heat the oil in a large frying pan and gently fry all the onions with the garlic for 5 minutes, until just softened. Using a draining spoon, place in the slow cooker dish.

3 Reheat the frying pan juices until hot and then stir-fry the beef for 5 minutes until sealed all over. Transfer the pan contents to the slow cooker dish, and add the bay leaves, pepper, cinnamon stick, vinegar and sugar, and mix well.

4 Mix the tomato purée into the chopped tomatoes and season with the salt. Pour over the beef, along with the wine, and mix well. Cover with the lid, switch the cooker on to Low, and cook for about 10 hours until tender. Discard the cinnamon stick, bay leaves and clove-studded onion.

5 Spoon over freshly cooked rice or hot cracked wheat and serve sprinkled with freshly chopped parsley. Accompany with a Greek-style salad.

COOK'S NOTE

Use 1 roughly chopped large onion if you don't want to spend time preparing small onions, and put the cloves into the sauce – remember to remove them before serving. If this dish sounds too fragrantly spicy for you, omit the cloves.

CHICKEN KORMA

Far nicer than anything you can get from the takeaway, there are quite a few ingredients involved, but the rewards are great.

PREPARATION
20 minutes + standing

COOKING TIME
15 minutes
+ 2 hours on High

SERVES 4

1 large onion
3 garlic cloves
2.5 cm (1 in) piece root ginger
675 g (1½ lb) skinless, boneless chicken
3 Tbsp ghee or 50 g (2 oz) butter
1 Tbsp ground coriander
1 small cinnamon stick, broken
5 cardamom pods, lightly crushed
Juice of 1 lemon

Salt and freshly ground black pepper
50 g (2 oz) ground almonds
50 g (2 oz) sultanas
200 ml (7 fl oz) canned coconut milk
100 ml (3½ fl oz) natural yoghurt
Freshly cooked basmati rice, to serve
Toasted flaked almonds and freshly
   chopped coriander, to serve
Cucumber, tomato and mint salad

1 Put the slow cooker on High to preheat for 20 minutes while you prepare the chicken.

2 Peel and roughly chop the onion, garlic and ginger. Put in a blender or food processor and blend for a few seconds until finely chopped.

3 Wash and pat dry the chicken, then cut into 2.5 cm (1 in) cubes. Heat the ghee or butter in a large frying pan until bubbling and fry the onion paste, stirring occasionally, for 10 minutes until softened but not brown. Add the chicken and continue to cook, stirring, for a further 5 minutes until sealed all over.

4 Transfer the frying pan contents to the slow cooker dish and add the spices, lemon juice and plenty of seasoning. Mix in the almonds, sultanas, coconut milk and yoghurt. Cover with the lid and cook for 2 hours until tender and cooked through. Discard the cinnamon stick and cardamom pods.

5 To serve, spoon over freshly cooked rice and sprinkle with toasted flaked almonds and chopped coriander. Accompany with a salad of chopped cucumber, tomato and mint.

COOK'S NOTE

Try using a combination of boneless leg and thigh meat with chicken breast for this dish; you'll find the dish has a more meaty flavour. Add 2 to 3 teaspoons of caster sugar to the mixture if you prefer a sweeter flavour.

A CLASSIC **CARBONNADE** OF BEEF

This French casserole always goes down well at a special occasion.
The mustardy toasts give the dish a delicious finishing touch.

PREPARATION
25 minutes

COOKING TIME
7 minutes
+ 1 hour on High
+ 6 hours on Low

SERVES 4

50 g (2 oz) butter
2 large onions
4 garlic cloves
1 Tbsp caster sugar
675 g (1½ lb) piece chuck or rump
   beef steak
Salt and freshly ground black pepper
1 Tbsp vegetable oil
2 Tbsp plain flour

300 ml (½ pt) hot beef stock
300 ml (½ pt) light ale or lager
Few sprigs of fresh thyme
1 bay leaf
1 small French stick
2 Tbsp Dijon mustard
50 g (2 oz) Gruyère cheese, grated
1 Tbsp freshly chopped thyme
Steamed asparagus, to serve

1 Put the butter in the slow cooker dish and cover with the lid. Switch on to the High setting and leave to preheat for 20 minutes while you prepare the vegetables.

2 Peel and chop the onions and garlic, then mix into the melted butter, along with the sugar. Cover and cook for 1 hour until softened but not browned. Mix well.

3 Just before the onions are ready, wash and pat dry the beef. Trim and cut into thin steaks, about 1 cm (½ in) thick. Season well.

4 Heat the oil in a large frying pan until hot and fry the steaks for 2 minutes on each side, until well sealed. Using tongs, arrange the steaks in the slow cooker dish, reserving the pan juices, and carefully mix with the onions. Re-cover.

5 Off the heat, mix the flour into the pan juices, and gradually blend in the hot stock and ale or lager. Pour the sauce over the steaks and add the herbs. Cover with the lid, reduce the setting to Low, and cook for about 6 hours until tender. Discard the herbs.

6 Just before serving, preheat the grill to a hot setting. Slice the bread into thin slices on the diagonal and toast for about 1 minute on each side. Spread one side of each slice with a little mustard and sprinkle with cheese. Grill for about 1 minute to melt the cheese. Sprinkle with thyme. Spoon the carbonnade on to warm serving plates and top with the cheesy toasts. Serve with steamed asparagus.

SUNDAY ROAST CHICKEN WITH SAGE AND ONION STUFFING

Browning the chicken is purely for the visual appearance of this dish;
it's up to you if you prefer to skip this step.

PREPARATION
20 minutes + standing

COOKING TIME
7 minutes
+ 3 hours on High

SERVES 4

1 small onion
1 Tbsp freshly chopped sage
   or 1 tsp dried
50 g (2 oz) fresh white breadcrumbs
Salt and freshly ground black pepper
1.35 kg (3 lb) oven-ready free-range
   chicken
1 small lemon

40 g (1½ oz) butter
1 Tbsp vegetable oil
6 rashers rindless smoked streaky
   bacon
12 cocktail-size pork sausages
Fresh sage and lemon wedges,
   to garnish
Freshly cooked vegetables, to serve

1 Put the slow cooker on High to preheat for 20 minutes while you prepare the chicken.

2 Peel and finely chop the onion. Place in a small heatproof bowl, along with the sage and breadcrumbs. Season well and set aside. Wash and pat dry the chicken. Season all over. Halve the lemon and insert in the central chicken cavity.

3 Heat the butter with the oil in a large frying pan until hot and bubbling. Put the chicken in the pan, breast-side down, so that it sits on one side. Cook for 2 minutes until lightly golden, then transfer to the other side and cook for a further 2 minutes. Drain the chicken, reserving the juices, and transfer to a heatproof plate.

4 Slice each bacon rasher in half lengthways to make two long strips, and wrap each piece around a sausage. Reheat the pan juices and brown the sausages for about 3 minutes, turning carefully, until lightly browned. Drain the sausages, reserving the pan juices, and set aside.

5 Mix the pan juices into the breadcrumbs to make a stuffing and push inside the neck end of the chicken. Fold the skin underneath the chicken and place in the slow cooker dish. Arrange the sausages around the chicken. Cover the top of the dish with a layer of foil, shiny-side down, and then cover with the lid. Cook for about 3 hours, or until the juices run clear (the internal temperature should read 80°C/176°F using a food probe).

6 Carefully remove the lid and foil, then drain the chicken and sausages, and stand on a warm serving platter. Re-cover with the foil and stand for 15 minutes. Discard the lemon. To serve, garnish the platter with fresh sage and wedges of lemon, and serve with freshly cooked vegetables. The cooking juices can be served as a gravy if desired.

OXTAIL IN RICH RED WINE AND ORANGE SAUCE

Oxtail is another cut that has made a comeback in recent years. It's cheap but the flavour is very beefy and the texture is meltingly tender.

PREPARATION
15 minutes

COOKING TIME
15 minutes
+ 6 hours on Low

SERVES 4

1.5 kg (3 lb 5 oz) oxtail pieces
3 Tbsp plain flour
Salt and freshly ground black pepper
1 large onion
450 g (1 lb) carrots
3 Tbsp vegetable oil
4 strips of orange rind
2 bay leaves

600 ml (1 pt) hot beef stock
300 ml (½ pt) dry red wine
1 Tbsp dark brown sugar
150 ml (¼ pt) freshly squeezed
   orange juice
Steamed rice and freshly cooked
   vegetables, to serve

1 Wash and pat dry the oxtail pieces. Place in a large bowl and toss in the flour and plenty of seasoning. Peel and slice the onion and cut the carrots in rounds.

2 Heat the oil in a large frying pan and gently fry the oxtail pieces in two batches, reserving the residual flour in the bowl, for 5 minutes, turning, until sealed all over. Using tongs or a draining spoon, transfer to the slow cooker dish and add the orange rind and bay leaves.

3 Reheat the frying pan juices until hot, and stir-fry the onion and carrots for 5 minutes. Remove from the heat and stir in the flour, then gradually blend in the hot stock, wine and sugar.

4 Pour into the slow cooker dish over the oxtail pieces, and mix in the orange juice. Cover with the lid, switch the cooker on to Low and cook for about 6 hours until tender and the meat falls off the bones. Discard the orange rind and bay leaves.

5 To serve, spoon over rice and serve with freshly cooked vegetables.

SPANISH-STYLE BEEF WITH BLACK BEANS AND CHORIZO

Chorizo sausage gives this dish a smoky spiciness that makes this stew the perfect meal for a chilly evening. Use haricot or kidney beans if black ones aren't available.

PREPARATION
20 minutes

COOKING TIME
20 minutes
+ 10 hours on Low

SERVES 4

150 g (5½ oz) dried black beans, soaked overnight
675 g (1½ lb) stewing beef
1 Tbsp sherry or white wine vinegar
1 tsp caster sugar
Salt and freshly ground black pepper
175 g (6 oz) chorizo sausage
1 large onion
2 garlic cloves

2 red peppers
2 Tbsp vegetable oil
2 tsp smoked paprika
Few sprigs of fresh rosemary
2 Tbsp plain flour
500 ml (18 fl oz) hot beef stock
400 g (14 oz) can chopped tomatoes
Mashed potatoes and vegetables, to serve

1 Rinse and drain the beans. Put in a saucepan, cover with water and bring to the boil. Boil rapidly for 10 minutes (see page 10). Drain well and set aside.

2 Meanwhile, cut the beef into 2 cm (¾ in) thick pieces and put in a bowl. Mix in the sherry or vinegar, sugar and plenty of seasoning. Set aside while preparing the rest of the dish.

3 Peel away the papery casing from the chorizo sausage and slice thinly. Peel and chop the onion and garlic. Deseed and chop the peppers.

4 Heat the oil in a large frying pan and gently fry the chorizo with the vegetables for 5 minutes, until just softened. Using a draining spoon, place in the slow cooker dish and add the paprika, beans and some rosemary. Mix well.

5 Mix the flour into the beef. Reheat the frying pan juices until hot and then stir-fry the flour-coated beef for 5 minutes until sealed all over. Transfer the pan contents to the slow cooker dish and mix well.

6 Pour over the hot stock and mix in the tomatoes. Cover with the lid, switch the cooker on to Low, and cook for about 10 hours until tender. Discard the rosemary.

7 To serve, spoon over creamy mashed potatoes and serve with your choice of freshly cooked vegetables.

PINTADE (GUINEA FOWL) VERONIQUE

Guinea fowl has a firmer texture and meatier flavour than chicken meat, but the recipe works just as well with chicken portions or even pheasant, if you prefer.

PREPARATION
20 minutes

COOKING TIME
10 minutes
+ 3 hours on High

SERVES 4

1 small onion
2 garlic cloves
1 guinea fowl
Salt and freshly ground black pepper
25 g (1 oz) butter
1 Tbsp olive oil
25 g (1 oz) plain flour
1 bay leaf

300 ml (½ pt) hot chicken stock
150 ml (¼ pt) dry white wine
175 g (6 oz) seedless green grapes
2 Tbsp freshly chopped tarragon
4 Tbsp double cream
Fresh tarragon, to garnish
French fries and a crisp salad, to serve

1 Put the slow cooker on High to preheat for 20 minutes while you prepare the guinea fowl.

2 Peel and chop the onion and garlic. Quarter the guinea fowl, then wash, pat dry and season all over. Heat the butter with the oil in a large frying pan until bubbling, and fry the guinea fowl pieces for 5 minutes, turning, until lightly golden all over. Drain, reserving the pan juices, and set aside.

3 Reheat the pan juices and cook the onion and garlic, stirring, for 5 minutes. Stir in the flour and bay leaf. Remove from the heat, and gradually stir in the hot stock and wine. Season with black pepper.

4 Arrange the guinea fowl pieces in the slow cooker dish, pour over the hot sauce and cover with the lid. Cook for 2 hours.

5 Wash and pat dry the grapes. Remove the guinea fowl from the slow cooker dish and set aside. Mix the grapes into the sauce, along with the tarragon and cream. Put the guinea fowl back in the dish, the other way up, re-cover, and cook for a further hour until the guinea fowl is tender and cooked through (the internal temperature should read 80°C/176°F using a food probe). Discard the bay leaf.

6 To serve, spoon on to warm serving plates, remove the skin if preferred, and garnish with tarragon. Accompany with French fries and a crisp salad.

SLOW-BRAISED DUCK WITH PINEAPPLE AND CHILLI SALSA

There's a bit of advance preparation to make sure the duck cooks just right, but otherwise this is a very simple recipe.

PREPARATION
25 minutes + salting and overnight drying

COOKING TIME
2 minutes
+ 2 hours on High
+ 25 minutes
optional roasting

SERVES 4

4 free-range duck legs
1 tsp salt
1 tsp caster sugar
3–4 sticks celery
1 tsp Chinese five-spice powder

Small bunch of fresh coriander
½ ripe medium-size pineapple
1 hot red chilli
Freshly cooked egg noodles, to serve

1 Wash the duck and dry thoroughly. Arrange on a plate. Mix the salt and sugar together and sprinkle over the skin of each duck leg. Leave uncovered in the fridge for 5 hours, then blot thoroughly with kitchen paper and place on a dry plate. Put back in the fridge and leave overnight to allow the skin to dry.

2 The next day, trim the celery and cut into suitable lengths to fit neatly inside the bottom of the slow cooker dish. You are aiming to form a fragrant 'rack' to imbue the duck and at the same time allow the juices to drain away. Preheat the cooker on High for 20 minutes while you finish preparing the duck.

3 Blot the duck skin again with kitchen paper. Season all over with five-spice powder. Heat a large frying pan until very hot, and put the duck into the pan, skin-side down. Cook for 2 minutes until richly browned. Drain, blot the duck skin and set aside.

4 Reserving a few sprigs of coriander, lay the rest on top of the vegetable rack. Arrange the duck pieces, side by side, on top. Cover with the lid and cook for 2 hours, until the duck is tender and cooked through (the internal temperature should read 80°C/176°F using a food probe). Drain well, discard the celery and coriander, and keep warm.

5 If you want crispy duck skin, preheat a conventional oven to 200°C/400°F (gas 6). Put the duck on a roasting rack over a tin and bake in the oven for 25 minutes until crispy and golden. Drain well.

6 Meanwhile, peel and core the pineapple. Finely chop the flesh and place in a bowl. Deseed and finely chop the chilli. Mix into the pineapple, then cover and chill until required.

7 To serve, pile some pineapple salsa on to warm serving plates and top each with a duck leg. Tear up the rest of the coriander and sprinkle on top. Serve with noodles.

CHICKEN WITH **40 GARLIC CLOVES**

The first time I tried this recipe it was out of sheer curiosity but at the same time with some trepidation. I hope you'll be as pleasantly surprised as I was!

PREPARATION
20 minutes + standing

COOKING TIME
4 minutes
+ 3 hours on High

SERVES 4

1.35 kg (3 lb) oven-ready free-range chicken
Salt and freshly ground black pepper
1 small bunch each of chervil, tarragon, parsley and thyme
2 bay leaves
1 large fennel bulb

4 Tbsp olive oil
40 garlic cloves, unpeeled
1 Tbsp fennel seeds, toasted
40 g (1½ oz) butter
Slices of lightly toasted French stick
Fresh herbs, to garnish

1 Put the slow cooker on High to preheat for 20 minutes while you prepare the chicken.

2 Wash and pat dry the chicken. Season all over. Put a few sprigs of each herb, along with one of the bay leaves in the central chicken cavity and set aside. Tie the remaining herbs together with a clean piece of string.

3 Trim the fennel, reserving the wispy fronds, then cut into thin slices and place in a large bowl. Gently mix in 3 tablespoons of the oil, the garlic cloves and toasted fennel seeds. Season well.

4 Heat the butter with the remaining oil in a large frying pan until hot and bubbling. Put the chicken in the pan, breast-side down, so that it sits on one side. Cook for 2 minutes until lightly golden, then cook on the other side for a further 2 minutes.

5 Put half the fennel and garlic mixture in the slow cooker dish. Drain the chicken, reserving the juices, and place on top. Spoon over the remaining fennel mixture and make sure the lid fits. Spoon over the reserved pan juices and lay the bunch of herbs on top of the chicken.

6 Cover the top of the dish with a layer of foil, shiny-side down, and then cover with the lid. Cook for about 3 hours, or until the juices run clear (the internal temperature should read 80°C/176°F using a food probe). Carefully remove the lid and foil, then drain the chicken and stand on a warm serving platter. Cover with foil and stand for 15 minutes. Drain the vegetables and keep warm. Discard the herbs.

7 To serve, slice the chicken and serve with the garlic and fennel. Accompany with toasted bread and garnish with fresh herbs and the reserved fennel fronds. Note: the garlic cooks to a molten paste which is very tasty smeared onto the toasted bread.

VENISON WITH BRAMBLES AND WHISKY

A few tastes from the Scottish Highlands presented in one dish. Raspberries work just as well, and you can replace the whisky with brandy for an alternative flavour.

PREPARATION
15 minutes

COOKING TIME
7 minutes
+ 4½ hours on Low

SERVES 4

4 slightly under-ripe pears
2 Tbsp light brown sugar
6 Tbsp whisky
600 g (1 lb 5 oz) stewing venison,
    such as boneless shoulder
1 large onion
25 g (1 oz) butter

3 Tbsp plain flour
450 ml (¾ pt) hot beef stock
300 ml (½ pt) pear or apple juice
2 bay leaves
Salt and freshly ground black pepper
225 g (8 oz) blackberries
Boiled pearl barley, to serve

1 Core and peel the pears, then cut into quarters. Arrange in the slow cooker dish, sprinkle with sugar and spoon over the whisky. Set aside.

2 Wash and pat dry the venison, and cut into 2.5 cm (1 in) pieces. Peel and chop the onion.

3 Melt the butter in a large frying pan until bubbling and gently fry the onion with the venison, stirring, for 5 minutes, until browned all over. Using a slotted spoon, transfer the venison and onion to the slow cooker dish.

4 Stir the flour into the reserved pan juices and gradually blend in the hot stock. Heat, stirring, until thickened. Remove from the heat and stir in the pear or apple juice. Pour over the venison, add the bay leaves and season well. Cover with the lid, switch the cooker on to Low, and cook for 4 hours until the venison is tender.

5 Wash and pat dry the blackberries and stir into the casserole. Re-cover and cook for a further 30 minutes, until the berries have softened. Discard the bay leaves.

6 To serve, ladle on to warm serving plates. Try serving with boiled pearl barley to accompany for a final Scottish flourish.

COOK'S NOTE

Venison is a very lean meat with little fat. You'll find cuts that are suitable for quick pan cooking as well as meat from parts of the animal that work hard like the shoulder and leg. Always choose the latter for long, slow cooking.

PHEASANT WITH JUNIPER-SCENTED RED CABBAGE

Juniper is a pungent spice, and a little goes a long way. It makes an ideal accompaniment for richer meats like game. Serve this braised dish simply with mashed sweet potato.

PREPARATION
20 minutes

COOKING TIME
4 minutes
+ 3 hours on Low

SERVES 4

350 g (12½ oz) red cabbage
1 red onion
2 eating apples
2 Tbsp raspberry or other fruit vinegar
50 g (2 oz) sultanas
50 g (2 oz) caster sugar
8 juniper berries, crushed

150 ml (¼ pt) dry red wine
4 boneless, skinless pheasant breasts
Salt and freshly ground black pepper
8 rashers rindless smoked streaky bacon
25 g (1 oz) butter
2 Tbsp freshly chopped parsley
Sweet potato mash, to serve

1 Put the slow cooker on High to preheat for 20 minutes while you prepare the cabbage and pheasant.

2 Trim and finely shred the cabbage. Place in a large bowl. Peel and finely slice the onion and mix into the cabbage. Peel and core the apples and chop finely. Mix into the cabbage, along with the vinegar, sultanas, sugar, juniper berries and wine. Set aside.

3 Wash and pat dry the pheasant breasts and season all over. Wrap two rashers of bacon, overlapping, around each breast and secure with a cocktail stick. Heat the butter in a frying pan until hot and bubbling, and fry the pheasant breasts for about 2 minutes on each side, until lightly browned. Set aside in the pan.

4 Pile the contents of the cabbage bowl into the slow cooker dish and arrange the pheasant breasts on top. Spoon over the pan juices and season again. Cover with the lid, reduce the setting to Low, and cook for 3 hours until both the cabbage and pheasant are tender and cooked through.

5 To serve, drain the cabbage, pile on to warm serving plates and sprinkle with parsley. Top each portion with a pheasant breast, removing the cocktail sticks. Accompany with mashed sweet potato – the cooking juices can be served as a sauce, if liked.

PORK AND SUN-DRIED TOMATO **ROLLS**

A combination of Italian flavours which turn a few simple ingredients into
a real feast. Use boneless chicken breasts if preferred.

PREPARATION
20 minutes

COOKING TIME
5 minutes
+ 4 hours on Low

SERVES 4

450 g (1 lb) piece pork fillet
Salt and freshly ground black pepper
6 Tbsp sun-dried tomato purée
6 Tbsp freshly grated Parmesan cheese
12 large sage leaves
6 wafer-thin slices Parma ham
1 medium onion

4 rashers rindless smoked streaky
    bacon
25 g (1 oz) butter
1 bay leaf
350 g (12½ oz) frozen peas, thawed
150 ml (¼ pt) dry vermouth

1 Put the slow cooker on High to preheat for 20 minutes while you prepare the pork.

2 Wash and pat dry the pork. Slice down the length of the fillet, cutting three-quarters of the way through. Lay the pork out on the work surface, cover with a sheet of plastic wrap, and bash with a rolling pin or meat cleaver to thin the meat to a thickness of about 5 mm (¼ in).

3 Remove the plastic wrap, season all over and spread with the tomato purée. Sprinkle with the cheese, then carefully roll up from one of the longer sides, tightly, like a Swiss roll. Cut in half to make two equal portions.

4 Wrap sage leaves round each piece of fillet and then wrap in Parma ham, securing with cocktail sticks. Set aside.

5 Peel and chop the onion. Chop the bacon. Melt the butter in a frying pan until bubbling and hot and fry the onion and bacon for 5 minutes, until lightly golden. Transfer to the slow cooker dish, along with the pan juices.

6 Add the bay leaf and lay the pork pieces on top. Cover the top of the dish with a layer of foil, shiny-side down, and then cover with the lid. Reduce the setting to Low and cook for 3 hours. Carefully remove the lid and foil, remove the pork and set aside. Stir in the thawed peas, vermouth and plenty of seasoning. Replace the pork on top, re-cover with the lid only, and continue to cook for a further hour until the pork is completely cooked through. Discard the bay leaf.

7 To serve, drain the pork and remove the cocktail sticks. Slice thinly. Drain the peas and place on to warm serving plates. Top with pork slices and serve immediately.

MUTTON AND PRUNE **TAGINE**

The conical lid of the Moroccan tagine is designed to retain all the cooking steam which helps cook meat to a mouth-watering tenderness. The slow cooker works in exactly the same way. Use lamb or stewing beef if preferred.

PREPARATION
20 minutes

COOKING TIME
10 minutes
+ 6 hours on Low

SERVES 4

Pinch of saffron strands
2 garlic cloves
1 large onion
750 g (1 lb 10 oz) stewing mutton
2 tsp each of ground cumin, coriander
    and ginger
1 tsp salt
Freshly ground black pepper

25 g (1 oz) butter
2 Tbsp olive oil
1 small cinnamon stick, broken
150 ml (¼ pt) freshly squeezed orange
    juice
250 g (9 oz) pitted prunes
Freshly cooked couscous, to serve
4 Tbsp freshly chopped coriander

1 Put the slow cooker on High to preheat for 20 minutes while you prepare the tagine.

2 Put the saffron in a small heatproof bowl and spoon over 2 tablespoons of hot water. Set aside to soak. Peel and finely chop the garlic and onion.

3 Trim away the excess fat from the mutton. Cut into 2.5 cm (1 in) thick pieces and put in a bowl. Mix in the garlic, ground spices, salt and pepper.

4 Heat the butter with the oil in a large frying pan until bubbling, and fry the onion for 5 minutes. Add the spiced mutton and cook, stirring, for about 5 minutes, until lightly browned all over.

5 Transfer all the pan contents to the slow cooker dish and mix in the saffron water, cinnamon stick and orange juice. Pour over 150 ml (¼ pt) hot water to barely cover the meat. Cover with the lid, reduce the setting to Low, and cook for 5 hours.

6 Remove the lid and stir in the prunes. Re-cover with the lid and continue to cook for a further hour until tender. Discard the cinnamon stick.

7 To serve, ladle the tagine over freshly cooked couscous and sprinkle with freshly chopped coriander.

KLEFTICO-STYLE **MUTTON**

The slow cooker is the perfect cooking vessel for mutton. A meat my grandmother used to cook, mutton is enjoying a bit of a resurgence. It has a stronger flavour than lamb, but lamb will cook in the same way if preferred.

PREPARATION
20 minutes + standing

COOKING TIME
10 minutes
+ 6 hours on Low

SERVES 4

1 small leg of mutton on the bone, weighing 1.35 kg (3 lb) – make sure the piece fits in your slow cooker
1 Tbsp olive oil
6 garlic cloves
2 onions

250 g (9 oz) ripe tomatoes
Small bunch of fresh oregano
Few sprigs of fresh rosemary
Salt and freshly ground black pepper
Freshly cooked rice or bulgar wheat and vegetables, to serve

1 Put the slow cooker on High to preheat for 20 minutes while you prepare the mutton.

2 Wash and pat dry the mutton. Heat the oil in a large frying pan until hot, then fry the mutton and cook for 5 minutes, turning the joint, until browned all over Drain the mutton, reserving the pan juices, and place on a heatproof plate.

3 Peel the garlic cloves, and cut them in half. Make small pockets in the mutton using a sharp knife and push a piece of garlic into each. Set aside. Peel and chop the onions. Roughly chop the tomatoes.

4 Reheat the pan juices and fry the onion for 5 minutes until lightly golden. Transfer the onion, along with the pan juices, to the slow cooker dish and mix in the tomatoes. Top with a few sprigs of the herbs and sit the mutton on top, pushing it down to ensure the lid will fit securely.

5 Season well and lay more herbs on top of the mutton. Cover the top of the dish with a layer of foil, shiny-side down, and then cover with the lid – this will ensure no moisture is lost and that the mutton cooks in its own juices. Reduce the setting to Low, and leave to cook for about 6 hours, until tender. Carefully remove the lid and foil, drain the mutton, place on a warm serving platter, cover with foil, and allow to stand for 15 minutes. Discard the cooking herbs.

6 To serve, skim off the fat, then push the cooking juices and vegetables through a nylon sieve. Carve the mutton and serve with the juices spooned over, accompanied with freshly cooked rice or bulgar wheat and vegetables.

LAMB **CASSOULET**

A hearty French classic ideally suited to the slow cooker. Use cubed pork or small chicken joints or pieces if preferred.

PREPARATION
10 minutes
+ overnight soaking

COOKING TIME
15 minutes
+ 7 hours on Low

SERVES 4

250 g (9 oz) dried haricot beans,
 soaked overnight
1 large onion
3 garlic cloves
500 g (1 lb 2 oz) lean lamb
175 g (6 oz) garlic sausage or chorizo
225 g (8 oz) ripe tomatoes
2 Tbsp olive oil

Few sprigs of fresh thyme and marjoram
1 bay leaf
150 ml (¼ pt) dry white wine
600 ml (1 pt) hot chicken stock
Salt and freshly ground black pepper
6 Tbsp fresh white breadcrumbs
2 Tbsp freshly chopped parsley

1 Rinse and drain the beans. Put in a saucepan, cover with water and bring to the boil. Boil rapidly for 10 minutes (see page 10). Drain well and put in the slow cooker dish.

2 Peel the onion and garlic, and chop finely. Wash and pat dry the lamb and cut into 2 cm (¾ in) thick cubes. Remove the skin or casing from the sausage or chorizo and cut into small pieces. Chop the tomatoes and set aside.

3 Heat the oil in a frying pan until hot and fry the onion, garlic, lamb and sausage, stirring for 5 minutes, until browned all over. Stir into the beans, along with the chopped tomatoes, herbs, wine and hot stock. Season well. Cover with the lid, switch the cooker on to Low and cook for about 7 hours until very tender.

4 Just before the end of cooking time, preheat the grill to its hottest setting. Line the grill tray with foil and spread the breadcrumbs on the foil evenly. Grill for about 1 minute, turning halfway, until lightly toasted and crisp.

5 To serve, spoon the cassoulet on to warm serving plates and sprinkle with crisp breadcrumbs and chopped parsley. Serve immediately.

COOK'S NOTE

Often a cassoulet is served on its own, but a crisp green salad makes a simple and fresh accompaniment.

SLOW-SIMMERED **SQUID** WITH **CHORIZO**

In order to enjoy squid at its best, you either need to cook it very quickly or very slowly. The latter means it absorbs all the flavours of the sauce it cooks in and becomes meltingly tender.

PREPARATION
20 minutes

COOKING TIME
6 minutes
+ 2 hours on Low

SERVES 4

Large pinch of saffron strands
450 g (1 lb) prepared whole squid
1 onion
2 garlic cloves
1 hot red chilli
175 g (6 oz) chorizo sausage
1 Tbsp olive oil
400 g can (14 oz) chickpeas, drained
  and rinsed

400 g (14 oz) can chopped tomatoes
1 tsp ground cumin
1 tsp caster sugar
Salt and freshly ground black pepper
150 ml (¼ pt) dry white wine
Steamed couscous and lemon zest,
  and crusty bread, to serve
Parsley sprigs, to garnish

1 Put the slow cooker on High to preheat for 20 minutes while you prepare the squid.

2 Put the saffron in a small heatproof bowl and spoon over 2 tablespoons of hot water. Set aside to soak.

3 Wash and pat dry the squid, then cut into squarish pieces about 5 cm (2 in) wide. Score each piece in a crisscross pattern on one side using a sharp knife. Set aside.

4 Peel and finely chop the onion and garlic. Deseed and finely chop the chilli. Peel away the papery casing from the chorizo and cut the sausage into small pieces. Heat the oil in a frying pan and stir-fry the chorizo for about 1 minute, until the juices start to run. Add the onion, garlic and chilli, and continue to stir-fry for a further 5 minutes.

5 Transfer the frying pan contents and juices to the slow cooker dish and mix in the squid, chickpeas, tomatoes, cumin, sugar and plenty of seasoning. Mix the wine in to the dish. Cover with the lid, reduce the heat to Low, and leave to cook for 2 hours until tender.

6 To serve, spoon the steamed couscous sprinkled with lemon zest on to warm dinner plates and spoon over the squid. Serve with crusty bread, garnish with parsley and serve immediately.

DUO OF **SALMON TERRINE** WITH ITALIAN FLAVOURS

This very fishy dish makes a stunning addition to a summer's meal – serve it in thicker slices with salad and new potatoes or cut more thinly and serve as a starter.

PREPARATION
20 minutes
+ cooling and chilling

COOKING TIME
3 hours on High

SERVES 8

350 g (12½ oz) thinly sliced smoked salmon
175 g (6 oz) roasted red peppers in oil, well drained
450 g (1 lb) fresh skinless salmon tail fillets
2 medium eggs
6 Tbsp double cream

4 Tbsp freshly grated Parmesan cheese
Salt and freshly ground black pepper
75 g (2½ oz) sun-dried tomatoes in oil, well drained
Small bunch of fresh basil
Wild rocket and chopped tomato salad, to serve

1 Put an upturned saucer or large metal pastry cutter in the bottom of the slow cooker dish and pour in sufficient hot water to come 5 cm (2 in) up the sides of the dish. Put the slow cooker on High to preheat for 20 minutes. Line a 900 g (2 lb) loaf tin with plastic wrap so that it overhangs the sides of the tin – make sure the tin fits in your slow cooker with the lid on.

2 Reserving two large slices of smoked salmon for later, line the sides and bottom of tin with the remaining slices. Slice the peppers and lay half in a layer at the bottom of the tin.

3 Wash and pat dry the salmon fillets. Cut into slices so that the salmon will fit along the length of the tin in two layers, then arrange half the cut salmon on top of the peppers in a single layer.

4 Put the eggs, cream, cheese and seasoning in a blender or food processor, along with the tomatoes and a few basil leaves. Blend for a few seconds.

5 Spoon on top of the salmon layer and arrange the remaining salmon slices in a layer on top, followed by a layer of the remaining peppers. Lay the reserved smoked salmon slices on top and fold the plastic wrap over the top.

6 Cover the top of the tin with a layer of foil for extra protection, sealing the edges well. Place the tin on the saucer or cutter, cover with the lid, and cook for 3 hours until set – a skewer inserted into the centre should come out clean. Remove the terrine from the slow cooker and drain off the juices. Stand, still covered, on a rack. Lay three heavy food cans on top and cool completely. Chill for at least 3 hours.

7 Remove the foil and invert the terrine on to a serving dish. Lift off the tin and peel away the plastic wrap. Stand at room temperature for 30 minutes, then slice and serve garnished with the remaining basil. Accompany with a rocket and tomato salad.

JUST PEACHY **POT ROAST HAM**

You can serve this dish straight from the cooker, unglazed, but I'm including the option of finishing it off in a conventional oven with a sweet fruity glaze. Serve hot or cold, as a roast or as part of a salad.

PREPARATION
20 minutes

COOKING TIME
5 hours on High
+ 40 minutes roasting

SERVES 6–8

1.5 kg (3 lb 5 oz) smoked boneless gammon joint, soaked overnight
1 onion
30–40 cloves
410 g (14½ oz) can peach halves in natural juice
2 bay leaves
3 Tbsp peach or other fruit chutney
3 Tbsp light brown sugar
2 ripe peaches, washed
15 g (½ oz) butter

1 Drain the gammon. Wash and pat dry, and place in the slow cooker dish to check that the lid will fit. Remove the gammon and set aside. Preheat the cooker on High for 20 minutes.

2 Peel the onion, cut in half and stud each half with three cloves. Set aside. Put the contents of the can of peaches in a blender or food processor and blend until smooth. Pour into the slow cooker dish.

3 Put the gammon back in the dish and arrange the onion halves and bay leaves around the meat. Add sufficient cold water to come two-thirds up the sides of the dish. Cover with the lid and cook for about 2 hours, then turn the gammon over and cook for a further 3 hours until tender and cooked through (the internal temperature should read 80°C/176°F using a food probe).

4 To serve the gammon unglazed, drain the meat and place on a serving platter. Serve hot or cold in slices.

5 To glaze the gammon, preheat a conventional oven to 200°C/400°F (gas 6). Drain the gammon, and place in a roasting tin. Discard the onion and bay leaves – use the cooking juices as stock for a soup.

6 Remove any string from the gammon and carefully slice off the brown rind, leaving a layer of white fat on the joint. Score the fat in a crisscross pattern and stud with the remaining cloves to decorate.

7 Mix the chutney and 2 tablespoons of the sugar together. Halve the peaches and remove the stones. Arrange around the gammon and dot each peach half with a little butter and sprinkle with the remaining sugar. Brush the chutney mixture over the gammon and bake in the oven for about 40 minutes, until richly golden.

8 To serve, drain the gammon and peaches and place on a warm serving platter. Slice and serve, hot or cold.

GOAT'S CHEESE AND SPINACH
CANNELLONI

I find it easier to make my own cannelloni tubes using sheets of lasagne which makes them more like pasta 'Swiss rolls'. Use ready-made tubes if you prefer.

PREPARATION
25 minutes

COOKING TIME
2 hours on Low

SERVES 4

12 sheets of fresh lasagne
350 g (12½ oz) frozen chopped spinach, thawed
2 spring onions
1 Tbsp cumin seeds, crushed
175 g (6 oz) firm goat's cheese
Salt and freshly ground black pepper

2 x 400 g (14 oz) cans chopped tomatoes with garlic
150 ml (¼ pt) dry white wine
150 g (5½ oz) mozzarella cheese
4 Tbsp freshly grated Parmesan cheese
Crisp salad, to serve

1 Put the slow cooker on High to preheat for 20 minutes while you prepare the cannelloni.

2 Half fill a heatproof bowl with boiling water and dip each sheet of lasagne, one at a time, in the water for a few seconds until pliable. Drain and lay them out on a clean, damp tea towel. Cover with a layer of plastic wrap and set aside.

3 Drain the spinach thoroughly and place in a food processor. Trim and roughly chop the spring onions and put in the processor, along with the cumin, goat's cheese and plenty of seasoning. Blend for a few seconds to make a smooth, thickish paste.

4 Remove the plastic wrap from the lasagne and spread a little of the paste over each sheet of lasagne. Roll up each sheet from one of the short ends, tightly, like a mini Swiss Roll.

5 Pour one can of tomatoes into the slow cooker dish and stir in the wine. Arrange the pasta rolls, seam-side down and side by side as far as possible (depending on the shape of your cooker dish), in the sauce. Spoon over the remaining can of tomatoes. Break off pieces of mozzarella and drop on top. Cover with the lid, reduce the setting to Low, and cook for 2 hours until tender.

6 Just before the end of cooking, preheat the grill to its highest setting. Spread out the cheese in four equal rounds on foil and cook for about 1 minute until melted and golden. Cool until firm, then gently peel from the foil.

7 To serve, spoon the cannelloni on to warm serving dishes and top each portion with a Parmesan crisp. Serve with a crisp salad.

MEDITERRANEAN VEGETABLE AND RICE LAYER

You can transform this dish from a taste of the Med to a taste of the exotic by replacing the herbs with Indian or Middle Eastern spices.

PREPARATION
25 minutes

COOKING TIME
7 minutes
+ 3 hours on High

SERVES 4

1 small aubergine
1 Tbsp salt
1 small fennel bulb
1 large yellow or green courgette
1 large red pepper
1 medium red onion
2 garlic cloves
4 Tbsp olive oil

Small bunch of fresh basil
Small bunch of fresh oregano
Freshly ground black pepper
150 ml (¼ pt) dry white wine
300 ml (½ pt) hot vegetable stock
225 g (8 oz) easy-cook white rice
Fresh herbs, to garnish

1 Trim the aubergine, cut into slices about 1 cm (½ in) thick and then cut in quarters. Layer in a colander, sprinkling with the salt as you go. Put the colander in a large bowl and set aside for 20 minutes, then rinse the aubergine well and pat dry with kitchen paper. Meanwhile, put the slow cooker on High to preheat for 20 minutes while you prepare the rest of the dish.

2 Trim the fennel and slice thinly. Discard the fronds. Trim and slice the courgette. Deseed and slice the pepper. Peel and chop the onion and garlic.

3 Heat the oil in a large frying pan until hot and stir-fry the onion, garlic and peppers for about 5 minutes, until softened. Stir in the courgette and aubergine, and cook for a further 2 minutes. Remove from the heat. Roughly chop the herbs.

4 Put the vegetables in the bottom of the slow cooker dish. Sprinkle over the herbs and season with black pepper. Pour in the wine and hot stock, cover with the lid, and cook for 2 hours until almost tender.

5 Spread out the rice on top of the vegetables, re-cover and cook for a further hour until the rice is tender and most of the liquid has been absorbed.

6 To serve, spoon the rice and vegetables on to warm serving plates, garnish with fresh herbs and serve immediately.

ORCHARD FRUITS WITH HONEY, BAY AND VANILLA

Delicious warm or cold, a great way to enjoy these seasonal fruits at their best. Halved peaches and nectarines can also be cooked this way.

PREPARATION
20 minutes + standing

COOKING TIME
3 hours on Low

SERVES 4

2 ripe pears
Juice of 1 lemon
2 firm-textured eating apples,
    such as Cox's
4 ripe apricots, washed
4 ripe plums, washed

2 Tbsp soft honey
2 fresh bay leaves or 1 dried
1 vanilla pod, split lengthways
300 ml (½ pt) unsweetened apple juice
Whipped cream, yoghurt or custard,
    to serve

1 Put the slow cooker on High to preheat for 20 minutes while you prepare the fruit.

2 Peel, core and halve the pears, and place in a bowl. Gently toss in the lemon juice. Prepare the apples in the same way but cut into quarters and coat in lemon juice. Halve the apricots and plums and remove the stones.

3 Arrange the fruit in the bottom of the slow cooker dish and spoon over the honey. Add the bay leaves and vanilla pod, and pour over the apple juice. Cover with the lid, reduce the setting to Low, and cook for 3 hours, turning the fruit halfway through, until it is tender. Turn off the cooker and stand for 30 minutes to 1 hour to allow the flavours to develop.

4 To serve, discard the bay leaves or reserve for decoration if liked. Serve the fruit warm for the best flavour, or allow to cool completely. Spoon over the cooking juices and accompany with whipped cream, yoghurt or custard.

COOK'S NOTE

Use this method and these quantities to cook any combination of the fruits above. For a variation, cook just pears and apples with a cinnamon stick instead of the bay leaves, and use cranberry juice instead of apple juice.

MIXED BERRY AND LEMON **GRUNT**

Based on a traditional American family favourite. 'Grunt' is simply stewed fruit with a sweet dumpling-type mixture, but it's surprisingly light and quite delicious.

PREPARATION
15 minutes

COOKING TIME
2½ hours on High

SERVES 6

2 lemons
675 g (1½ lb) frozen mixed berries
150 g (5½ oz) caster sugar, plus 2 Tbsp
175 g (6 oz) self-raising flour,
  plus extra for dusting

75 g (2½ oz) vegetable suet
2 cardamom pods
About 100 ml (3½ fl oz) whole milk
2 Tbsp demerara sugar
Custard, cream or ice cream, to serve

1 Finely grate the rind from the lemons and put half in the slow cooker dish. Extract the juice and pour into the dish. Stir in the frozen berries and 150 g (5½ oz) of caster sugar.

2 Cover with the lid and switch the cooker on to High. Leave to cook for 1½ hours, until completely thawed and hot.

3 Just before the end of cooking time, make the dumplings. Sift the flour and stir in the suet, remaining 2 tablespoons of sugar and lemon rind. Peel the green casing from the cardamom pods and discard the casings. Finely grind the cardamom seeds. Add to the flour and stir in approximately 100 ml (3½ fl oz) milk to form a soft dough. Lightly dust your hands and work surface with a little more flour and knead the dough lightly. Divide into 12 equal portions.

4 Remove the lid and stir the fruit. Arrange the portions of dough round the edge of the dish on top of the fruit, re-cover, and continue to cook for a further hour until the dough portions have merged together and are cooked through. Sprinkle with demerara sugar.

5 Spoon into warm pudding bowls and serve immediately with custard, pouring cream or ice cream.

COOK'S NOTE

You can make this dish with any of your favourite fruit. Replace the lemon with orange juice or other fruit juice if you prefer. A pinch of nutmeg or cinnamon added to the dumpling mixture is good with pears, plums and apples.

TREACLE TART APPLES AND CUSTARD

Two desserts in one: soft, fluffy apples baked with a classic treacle tart filling, and with custard to finish. Perfect.

PREPARATION
20 minutes

COOKING TIME
2½ hours on Low
+ 15 minutes on High

SERVES 4

4 medium-size Bramley cooking apples
75 g (2½ oz) fresh white breadcrumbs
2 Tbsp golden syrup, plus extra to serve
40 g (1½ oz) butter
1 small unwaxed lemon
425 g (15 oz) can custard

1 Put the slow cooker on High to preheat for 20 minutes while you prepare the apples.

2 Remove the core from the apples using an apple corer, then wash and pat dry. Using a small sharp knife, lightly score a horizontal line around the middle of each apple to help prevent the skin splitting unevenly during cooking. Set aside.

3 Put the breadcrumbs in a heatproof bowl. Put the golden syrup and butter in a small saucepan and heat gently until melted. Finely grate 1 teaspoon of lemon rind into the breadcrumbs, then extract the juice into a separate bowl.

4 Stir 1 tablespoon of lemon juice into the breadcrumbs, along with the melted syrup mixture. Divide the mixture evenly between the apple cavities, packing the mixture down into each.

5 Line the bottom of the slow cooker dish with baking parchment and stand the apples side by side on top. Mix the remaining lemon juice with 2 tablespoons of hot water and pour into the dish. Cover with the lid, reduce the setting to Low, and cook for 2½ hours, until the apples are soft.

6 Carefully remove the apples and stir the custard into the cooking juices. Replace the apples. Cover with the lid, raise the setting to High, and cook for a further 15 minutes to warm the custard. Serve immediately with extra golden syrup to spoon over.

REAL VANILLA AND COFFEE **CUSTARDS**

A richly flavoured version of the classic egg custard dessert. Replace the espresso coffee with extra single cream if you prefer a plain custard.

PREPARATION
20 minutes
cooling and chilling

COOKING TIME
2½ hours on Low

MAKES 4

1 vanilla pod
150 ml (¼ pt) cold espresso or strong
  black coffee
250 ml (9 fl oz) single cream
3 Tbsp maple syrup
2 medium eggs, beaten
1 medium egg yolk
4 Tbsp whipped cream, to serve
Chocolate coffee beans, to decorate

1 Put the slow cooker on High to preheat for 20 minutes while you prepare the custards.

2 Lightly grease four 175 ml (6 fl oz) ovenproof teacups, ramekins or similar ovenproof dishes. The dishes will need to sit side by side in your slow cooker so make sure they fit.

3 Split the vanilla pod lengthways and scrape out the seeds from each half into a large jug. In another jug, pour in the coffee, cream, maple syrup, eggs and egg yolk. Mix well, then strain through a sieve into the jug with the vanilla.

4 Stand the dishes side by side in the bottom of the cooker dish. Mix the custard again and carefully pour sufficient into each dish to fill it to within 1 cm (½ in) from the rim.

5 Carefully pour in sufficient hot water to come halfway up the sides of the dishes, then lay a sheet of baking parchment on top to cover all four dishes. Cover with the lid, reduce the setting to Low, and cook for 2 to 2½ hours, until just set in the centre but still wobbly – a knife inserted into the centre will come out clean when the custards are set.

6 Remove from the slow cooker and allow to cool completely, then cover and chill for at least 2 hours. When ready to serve, top each with a spoonful of whipped cream and decorate with chocolate coffee beans.

FRUIT AND SPICE **BREAD AND BUTTER PUDDINGS**

Traditionally served hot with pouring cream, but also delicious chilled and served cold. Use plain white bread or brioche if preferred.

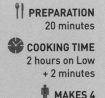

PREPARATION
20 minutes

COOKING TIME
2 hours on Low
+ 2 minutes

MAKES 4

50 g (2 oz) butter, softened
6 x 1 cm (½ in) thick slices cut from
   a small white fruit loaf
50 g (2 oz) mixed dried fruit
250 ml (9 fl oz) double cream
2 Tbsp caster sugar
2 medium eggs, beaten
1 tsp ground cinnamon
8 tsp demerara sugar

1 Put the slow cooker on High to preheat for 20 minutes while you prepare the puddings.

2 Grease four 10 cm (4 in) diameter ramekins or similar ovenproof dishes with a little of the butter. The dishes will need to sit side by side in your slow cooker so make sure they fit.

3 Slice the crusts off the bread if preferred, and butter each slice with the remaining butter. Sprinkle three slices evenly with dried fruit and then sandwich together with the remaining slices to make three fruity sandwiches. Cut each sandwich diagonally in quarters to make 12 small triangles.

4 Neatly arrange three triangular sandwiches per dish. Mix the cream with the caster sugar, eggs and cinnamon, and pour over the top, allowing the mixture to soak into the bread.

5 Stand the dishes side by side in the slow cooker dish, and carefully pour in sufficient hot water to come halfway up the sides of the dishes, then lay a sheet of baking parchment on top to cover all four dishes. Cover with the lid, reduce the setting to Low, and cook for 1½ to 2 hours, until just firm.

6 Preheat the grill to its hottest setting. Carefully remove the puddings from the cooker dish and stand on the grill tray. Sprinkle each with the sugar and cook for about 2 minutes, until golden and caramelized. Serve while hot.

COOK'S NOTE

For traditional non-fruited puddings, omit the fruit and cinnamon. Add a few drops of vanilla extract or ½ teaspoon of finely grated lemon rind for a citrus-flavoured custard.

WHITE CHOCOLATE **RISOTTO**

A contemporary twist on a traditional nursery pudding. A rice pudding is one of the easiest puddings you can make in a slow cooker; no preheating required, just an occasional stir.

PREPARATION
5 minutes

COOKING TIME
5 minutes
+ 3½ hours on Low

SERVES 4–6

40 g (1½ oz) butter
300 g (10½ oz) Arborio rice
1 L (1¾ pt) hot whole milk
3 Tbsp caster sugar
4 Tbsp double cream
100 g (3½ oz) white chocolate chips
1 tsp good-quality vanilla extract
2 tsp cocoa powder
Raspberries, to serve

1 Melt the butter in a saucepan and then add the rice, and cook, stirring for 1 minute, until the rice is buttery all over. Pour in a little of the hot milk and simmer gently until it is absorbed.

2 Transfer the rice mixture to the slow cooker dish and stir in the remaining milk and the sugar.

3 Cover with the lid, switch the cooker on to Low, and cook for 3½ hours, stirring occasionally, until the rice is tender, thick and creamy.

4 Stir in the cream, chocolate chips and vanilla. Serve immediately, spooned into warm serving bowls, and dust with cocoa powder. Accompany with raspberries.

COOK'S NOTE

This recipe also works well with plain or dark chocolate, but you can leave the chocolate out altogether for a plain pudding – why not try stirring in some cinnamon and dried fruit or some small, crushed fresh berries instead?

UPSIDE-DOWN BANANA AND GINGER **CHEESECAKE**

In this recipe, the biscuit base you usually associate with a cheesecake gets added afterwards and so becomes more like a crunchy topping.

PREPARATION
25 minutes
+ cooling and chilling

COOKING TIME
1 hour on High

SERVES 6

225 g (8 oz) full-fat soft cheese
1 medium-size ripe banana
1 piece stem ginger in syrup, together
   with 1 Tbsp syrup
1 large egg, beaten

50 g (2 oz) caster sugar
25 g (1 oz) butter, melted
100 g (3½ oz) ginger biscuits, crushed
Sliced banana and grated chocolate,
   to decorate

1 Put the slow cooker on High to preheat for 20 minutes while you prepare the cheesecake.

2 Grease and line a deep 15 cm (6 in) loose-bottomed round tin – the tin will need to sit in your slow cooker so make sure it fits. Wrap the outside of the tin with foil in order to make it watertight.

3 Put the soft cheese in a bowl and beat with a wooden spoon until soft and smooth. Peel and mash the banana. Finely chop the ginger. Stir both into the soft cheese, along with the ginger syrup, egg and sugar. Spoon the mixture into the prepared tin and smooth over the surface. Cover the top of the tin with plastic wrap.

4 Stand the tin in the cooker dish, and carefully pour in sufficient hot water to come halfway up the sides of the tin. Cover with the lid and cook on High for about 1 hour until the cheesecake is just set.

5 Once the cheesecake is cooked, carefully remove from the cooker, discard the plastic wrap and foil, and allow to cool completely. Melt the butter in a pan and stir into the crushed biscuits. Sprinkle evenly over the top and press down gently. Chill for at least 1 hour before carefully removing from the tin and serving decorated with sliced banana and grated chocolate.

COOK'S NOTE

If you prefer, make up the biscuit base and press into the bottom of the tin before you add the cheesecake mixture. Cook as above to give a soft-crusted base.

LAST-MINUTE BOOZY
CHRISTMAS PUDDING

Traditional festive puddings taste great but need to be made some time in advance. This one can be made much closer to the big day. It's fruity and packs a punch!

PREPARATION
20 minutes

COOKING TIME
2 hours on High

SERVES 8

200 g (7 oz) no-need-to-soak pitted prunes
Juice and finely grated rind of 1 small orange
6 Tbsp brandy
1 medium egg, beaten
150 g (5½ oz) mixed dried fruit

75 g (2½ oz) dark brown sugar
2 tsp mixed spice
100 g (3½ oz) ground almonds
40 g (1½ oz) fresh white breadcrumbs
40 g (1½ oz) shredded vegetable suet
Custard or single cream, to serve

1 Put the slow cooker on High to preheat for 20 minutes while you prepare the pudding. Grease a 600 ml (1 pt) pudding basin – make sure the basin fits in your slow cooker with the lid on.

2 Put the prunes in a blender or food processor with the orange juice and rind, along with 4 tablespoons of the brandy and the egg. Blend for a few seconds until smooth. Put the dried fruit, sugar, mixed spice, almonds, breadcrumbs and suet in a bowl, and mix in the blended prune mixture until well combined.

3 Spoon into the prepared basin and smooth over the top. Place a circle of baking parchment directly on top of the mixture, then cover the top of the basin loosely with a layer of pleated foil to allow the pudding to rise. Secure with string.

4 Stand the basin in the slow cooker dish and carefully pour in sufficient hot water to come halfway up the sides of the basin. Cover with the lid and cook on High for about 2 hours until firm. Test the centre with a skewer: if it comes out clean, the pudding is cooked.

5 Carefully remove the pudding from the slow cooker and unwrap. Invert on to a warm serving plate. Spoon over the remaining brandy and serve hot with custard or cream.

COOK'S NOTE

You can make the pudding up to five days in advance, just remove the wrappings and allow to cool in the basin, then cover and keep in the fridge. To reheat, preheat the slow cooker and re-cover the pudding as above. Stand in the cooker and add hot water as above. Cook on High for about 1 hour until piping hot.

SYRUP-DRENCHED CHERRY
SPONGE PUDDING

A yummy pudding for cold days. You can put your favourite jam at the bottom if you prefer, and add dried fruit instead of cherries.

PREPARATION
20 minutes + standing

COOKING TIME
1½ hours on High

SERVES 4–6

4 Tbsp golden syrup
115 g (4 oz) self-raising flour
50 g (2 oz) caster sugar
50 g (2 oz) glacé cherries, chopped
50 g (2 oz) shredded suet
Pinch of salt

Few drops of good-quality almond
   extract
1 medium egg, beaten
3–4 Tbsp whole milk
Custard, to serve

1 Put the slow cooker on High to preheat for 20 minutes while you prepare the pudding. Generously grease a 600 ml (1 pt) pudding basin – make sure the basin fits in your slow cooker with the lid on. Spoon 2 tablespoons of golden syrup into the bottom of the basin.

2 In a mixing bowl, sift the flour and stir in the sugar, cherries, suet and salt. Add a few drops of almond extract, and bind together with the egg and sufficient milk to make a smooth and spoonable batter.

3 Spoon into the prepared basin and smooth over the top. Place a circle of baking parchment on top of the mixture, then cover the top of the basin loosely with a layer of pleated foil to allow the pudding to rise. Secure with string.

4 Stand the basin in the slow cooker dish and carefully pour in sufficient hot water to come halfway up the sides of the basin. Cover with the lid and cook on High for about 1½ hours until risen and firm. Test the centre with a skewer: if it comes out clean, the pudding is cooked.

5 Carefully remove the pudding from the cooker and stand for 5 minutes before removing from the basin. Loosen the pudding around the edge with a palette knife, then carefully invert on to a serving plate – remember the syrup will be very hot. Spoon over the remaining syrup and serve immediately with custard.

FONDANT CHOCOLATE CARAMEL PUDDINGS

These tempting delights are definitely worth a try, whatever the occasion.
A guaranteed spoonful of comfort with every mouthful.

PREPARATION
20 minutes

COOKING TIME
40 minutes on High

MAKES 4

125 g (4½ oz) dark chocolate
125 g (4½ oz) unsalted butter
2 medium eggs, beaten
2 medium egg yolks
4 Tbsp caster sugar
8 squares chocolate-covered soft caramel bar
Single cream, to serve

1 Put the slow cooker on High to preheat for 20 minutes while you prepare the puddings.

2 Lightly grease and flour four 150 ml (¼ pt) pudding basins or similar ovenproof dishes. The basins will need to sit side by side in your slow cooker so make sure they fit.

3 Break the chocolate into pieces and place in a heatproof bowl. Cut the butter into small cubes and add to the chocolate. Set the bowl over a saucepan of gently simmering water and allow to melt. Remove from the water and cool for 5 minutes.

4 Meanwhile, whisk the eggs, egg yolks and sugar together until pale and foamy. Whisk in the warm melted chocolate mixture to make a thick batter.

5 Three-quarter fill the prepared basins with the chocolate mixture. Push two squares of the caramel bar into the centre of each pudding. Place a circle of baking parchment directly on top of the mixture of each basin.

6 Stand the basins side by side in the slow cooker dish and carefully pour in sufficient hot water to come halfway up the sides of the basins. Cover with the lid and cook on High for 40 minutes until risen and firm on top but still wobbly.

7 Carefully remove from the slow cooker dish. Discard the paper and immediately invert the puddings on to warm serving plates. Let stand upside down in their basins for 30 seconds before shaking gently to remove the basin. Serve immediately with cream.

VERY CHOCOLATEY **LOAF CAKE**

A rich-textured bake with chunks of chocolate to add to its decadence. If you can, keep for 24 hours before slicing – the flavour and texture will be even better!

PREPARATION
20 minutes + cooling

COOKING TIME
1½ hours on High

SERVES 6

115 g (4 oz) dark chocolate
115 g (4 oz) unsalted butter
100 g (3½ oz) dark brown sugar
2 medium eggs, beaten
75 g (2½ oz) self-raising flour
75 g (2½ oz) plain, milk or white
  chocolate chunks
1 tsp good quality vanilla extract

1 Put the slow cooker on High to preheat for 20 minutes while you prepare the cake. Grease and line a 450 g (1 lb) loaf tin – make sure the tin fits in your slow cooker with the lid on.

2 Break the dark chocolate into pieces and place in a heatproof bowl. Cut the butter into small chunks and add to the chocolate. Set the bowl over a saucepan of gently simmering water until melted. Remove from the water and cool for 10 minutes.

3 Stir the sugar and eggs into the chocolate mixture and sieve in the flour. Add the chocolate chunks and vanilla, and gently mix all the ingredients together.

4 Spoon the mixture into the prepared tin and smooth the top. Cover the surface with a piece of baking parchment and then cover the top of the tin loosely with a layer of pleated foil to allow the cake to rise. Stand the tin in the cooker dish and carefully pour in sufficient hot water to come halfway up the sides of the tin. Cover with the lid and cook on High for about 1½ hours until risen and firm. Test the centre with a skewer: if it comes out clean, the cake is cooked.

5 Remove from the cooker and stand on a wire rack. Allow to cool completely before removing from the tin, then wrap and store for 24 hours to allow the flavour and texture to develop. To serve, slice thickly and enjoy!

GINGER AND ORANGE **CAKE**

Another dense-textured bake which benefits from this type of cooking. The texture is dense and moist, and it keeps getting better the longer you store it.

 PREPARATION
20 minutes + cooling

COOKING TIME
2 hours on High

SERVES 6

75 g (2½ oz) treacle
75 g (2½ oz) golden syrup
75 g (2½ oz) dark brown sugar
75 g (2½ oz) butter or margarine
150 g (5½ oz) self-raising flour
2 tsp ground ginger
1 tsp mixed spice
75 ml (2½ fl oz) whole milk
½ tsp finely grated orange rind

1 Put an upturned saucer or large metal pastry cutter in the bottom of the slow cooker dish and pour in sufficient hot water to come 2.5 cm (1 in) up the sides of the cooker. Put the slow cooker on High to preheat for 20 minutes while you prepare the gingerbread. Grease and line a 450 g (1 lb) loaf tin – make sure the tin fits in your slow cooker with the lid on.

2 Put the treacle, golden syrup, sugar and butter or margarine in a small saucepan, and heat gently until melted together – do not allow it to get too hot. Sift the flour and spices into a bowl and make a well in the centre. Gradually stir in the melted ingredients with the milk and orange rind until well mixed.

3 Spoon the mixture into the prepared tin, smooth the top, and cover the surface with a piece of baking parchment. Cover the top of the tin loosely with a layer of pleated foil to allow the cake to rise. Stand the tin on the saucer or cutter in the cooker dish. Cover with the lid and cook on High for about 2 hours until risen and firm. Test the centre with a skewer: if it comes out clean, the cake is cooked.

4 Remove from the slow cooker, discard the paper and foil, and stand on a wire rack. Allow to cool completely before removing from the tin – the cake may sink slightly on cooling. Wrap and store for 24 hours to allow the flavour and texture to develop. To serve, slice thickly and either serve plain or spread with butter or soft cheese.

MOCHA PEAR **UPSIDE-DOWN CAKE**

Serve this one up for pudding, hot with custard, or allow to cool and it makes a lovely slice to have with morning coffee.

PREPARATION
20 minutes + cooling

COOKING TIME
1½ hours on High

SERVES 6

2 medium-size ripe pears
115 g (4 oz) butter or margarine, softened
115 g (4 oz) light brown sugar
2 medium eggs, beaten
115 g (4 oz) self-raising flour
15 g (½ oz) cocoa powder
2 Tbsp cold, very strong black coffee

1 Put an upturned saucer or large metal pastry cutter in the bottom of the slow cooker dish and pour in sufficient hot water to come 2.5 cm (1 in) up the sides of the cooker. Put the slow cooker on High to preheat for 20 minutes while you prepare the cake. Grease and line a deep 15 cm (6 in) round cake tin – make sure the tin fits in your slow cooker with the lid on.

2 Peel and core the pears, then slice in quarters and arrange over the bottom of the tin. Set aside.

3 In a mixing bowl, cream together the butter or margarine and sugar until pale and creamy. Gradually whisk in the eggs. Sift the flour and cocoa powder into the bowl, and carefully fold into the mixture, along with the coffee.

4 Spoon into the prepared tin and smooth the mixture carefully over the pears. Place a circle of baking parchment directly on top of the cake mixture. Cover the top of the tin loosely with a layer of pleated foil to allow the cake to rise. Stand the tin on the saucer or pastry cutter. Cover with the lid and cook on High for about 1½ hours until risen and firm. Test the centre with a skewer: if it comes out clean, the cake is cooked.

5 Remove the cake from the slow cooker and stand on a wire rack. Either turn out immediately to serve as a pudding or allow to cool completely before removing from the tin. Serve upside down, with the pears on top.

PASSIONATE CARROT AND WALNUT CAKE

Passion cake and carrot cake have become a mainstay on tea shop menus everywhere. This version is perfect for slow cooking.

⏲ PREPARATION
25 minutes + cooling

🕐 COOKING TIME
1½ hours on High

👤 SERVES 6

150 g (5½ oz) butter or margarine, softened
115 g (4 oz) light brown sugar
2 medium eggs, beaten
50 g (2 oz) sultanas
100 g (3½ oz) finely chopped walnuts
75 g (2½ oz) grated carrot

115 g (4 oz) wholemeal self-raising flour
1 tsp ground mixed spice, plus extra for dusting
125 g (4½ oz) full-fat soft cheese
2 Tbsp icing sugar
Few drops of vanilla extract

1 Put an upturned saucer or large metal pastry cutter in the bottom of the slow cooker dish and pour in sufficient hot water to come 2.5 cm (1 in) up the sides of the cooker. Put the slow cooker on High to preheat for 20 minutes while you prepare the cake. Grease and line a deep 15 cm (6 in) round cake tin – make sure the tin fits in your slow cooker with the lid on.

2 In a mixing bowl, cream together 115 g (4 oz) of the butter or margarine with the sugar until pale and creamy. Gradually whisk in the eggs and stir in the sultanas, 50 g (2 oz) of the walnuts and the grated carrot.

3 Sift the flour and 1 teaspoon of mixed spice on top, adding any husks that remain in the sieve, and carefully fold into the cake mixture. Spoon into the prepared tin and smooth the top. Place a circle of baking parchment directly on top of the cake mixture and cover the top of the tin loosely with a layer of pleated foil to allow the cake to rise.

4 Stand the tin on the saucer or pastry cutter, cover with the lid and cook on High for about 1½ hours until risen and firm. Test the centre with a skewer: if it comes out clean, the cake is cooked.

5 Remove the cake from the cooker and stand on a wire rack. Allow to cool completely before removing from the tin. Wrap and store for 24 hours to allow the flavour and texture to develop.

6 To serve, beat the soft cheese and remaining butter together until smooth. Sift the icing sugar on top, add a few drops of vanilla extract and mix well. Spread over the top of the cake and sprinkle with the remaining chopped walnuts and extra mixed spice if liked.

BANANA, CARDAMOM AND COCONUT **LOAF**

Half cake, half bread, this moist loaf can be eaten plain, spread with butter or iced with your favourite topping – it's delicious with chocolate spread!

PREPARATION
25 minutes
+ cooling and setting
 	
COOKING TIME
1 hour on High
 	
SERVES 6
	175 g (6 oz) self-raising flour
	¼ tsp ground cardamom
	50 g (2 oz) caster sugar
	50 g (2 oz) unsweetened desiccated
	   coconut
	50 ml (2 fl oz) sunflower oil
	
	1 large egg, beaten
	100 ml (3½ fl oz) canned coconut milk,
	   plus 1 Tbsp
	1 medium-size ripe banana
	75 g (2½ oz) icing sugar
	1 Tbsp toasted desiccated coconut

1 Put the slow cooker on High to preheat for 20 minutes while you prepare the loaf. Grease and line a 450 g (1 lb) loaf tin – make sure the tin fits in your slow cooker with the lid on.

2 Sieve the flour and cardamom into a mixing bowl and stir in the sugar and desiccated coconut. Make a well in the centre and add the oil and egg. Mix well, along with 100 ml (3½ fl oz) coconut milk to form a thick batter.

3 Peel and mash the banana and fold into the batter. Spoon the mixture into the prepared tin, smooth the top and cover the surface with a piece of baking parchment. Cover the top of the tin loosely with a layer of pleated foil to allow the loaf to rise, and stand the tin in the slow cooker dish. Pour in sufficient hot water to come halfway up the sides of the tin. Cover with the lid and cook on High for about 1 hour until risen and firm. Test the centre with a skewer: if it comes out clean, the cake is cooked.

4 Remove the loaf from the cooker, discard the paper and foil, and stand on a wire rack. Allow to cool completely before removing from the tin. Wrap and store for 24 hours to allow the flavour and texture to develop.

5 When ready to serve, sieve the icing sugar into a bowl and mix in the remaining tablespoon of coconut milk to make a smooth icing. Spread over the loaf and sprinkle with toasted desiccated coconut. Stand for a few minutes to set before slicing to serve.

COOK'S NOTE

Try this loaf un-iced served hot as a pudding, with chocolate ice cream or custard.

SWEET, SPICY CHERRY TOMATO AND ONION **RELISH**

A tangy condiment perfect for pepping up a sandwich filling or for serving with cold meats and cheeses

PREPARATION
20 minutes + cooling

COOKING TIME
6½ hours on High

MAKES
about 1.5 kg (3 lb 5oz)

900 g (2 lb) ripe cherry tomatoes
900 g (2 lb) red or white onions
4 garlic cloves
1 hot red chilli
4 Tbsp cold-pressed rapeseed oil,
   or other vegetable oil
Few sprigs of fresh rosemary

1 bay leaf
175 g (6 oz) light brown sugar
6 Tbsp balsamic vinegar
50 g (2 oz) sultanas
1 tsp salt
Freshly ground black pepper

1 Put the slow cooker on High to preheat for 20 minutes while you prepare the relish.

2 Remove the stalks from the tomatoes, then wash, pat dry and quarter. Peel the onions and slice thinly. Peel and crush the garlic. Deseed and finely chop the chilli.

3 Put the prepared vegetables in the slow cooker dish and mix in the oil and herbs. Cover with the lid and cook on High for about 4 hours, stirring occasionally, until very soft.

4 Stir in the remaining ingredients and cook, uncovered, for a further 2½ hours, stirring occasionally, until the mixture is thick and jam-like. Switch off the slow cooker and allow to cool completely in the cooker.

5 Discard the rosemary and bay leaf. Spoon the relish into prepared sterilized jars (see page 151) and seal with waxed paper discs and jam pot covers or non-corrosive lids. Store in the fridge for up to three months. Once opened, keep in the fridge and use within a month.

COOK'S NOTE

For a less spicy version, omit the chilli, and for a different flavour, try adding 2 teaspoons of smoked paprika.

The relish will become very hot during cooking, so make sure the cooker is positioned where it will stay undisturbed.

CHILLI, PEPPER AND MANGO **CHUTNEY**

No Indian meal would be complete without this most well-known of Asian preserves. Mango chutney makes an ideal accompaniment to Christmas leftovers too!

PREPARATION
25 minutes + cooling

COOKING TIME
5 hours on High

MAKES
1 kg (2 lb 3 oz)

3 firm mangoes
1 large red pepper
1 hot red chilli
2 garlic cloves
2.5 cm (1 in) piece root ginger
Seeds from 4 cardamom pods
1 tsp cumin seeds

1 tsp coriander seeds
300 ml (½ pt) white wine vinegar
300 g (10½ oz) caster sugar
1 tsp salt
Freshly ground black pepper
2 tsp black onion seeds

1 Slice down either side of the smooth, central stone of the mango, remove the skin and finely chop the flesh – you should end up with about 750 g (1 lb 10 oz) mango flesh. Put in the slow cooker dish.

2 Halve, deseed and finely chop the pepper and chilli. Peel and crush the garlic cloves, and peel and finely chop the ginger. Mix into the chopped mango. Put all the spice seeds in a pestle and mortar and finely crush, then add to the mixture.

3 Pour over the vinegar and mix well. Cover with the lid, put the slow cooker on High, and cook for 2 hours, stirring halfway through. Stir in the sugar until dissolved, then leave to cook, uncovered, for about 3 hours, stirring occasionally, until thick and jam-like. Season and stir in the onion seeds.

4 Switch off the slow cooker, remove the lid, and cover loosely with kitchen paper or a clean tea towel. Allow to cool completely.

5 Spoon the chutney into cold, sterilized jars (see page 151). Cover the top with waxed paper discs and then seal with a transparent jam cover or screw-on lid. Store in the fridge for at least one week before eating, or for up to three months. Once opened, keep in the fridge and use within a month.

COOK'S NOTE

The chutney will become very hot during cooking, so make sure the cooker is positioned where it will stay undisturbed.

PRESERVING TIPS AND TECHNIQUES

Sterilizing jars: wash undamaged jars thoroughly in very hot water with mild detergent and rinse well. Place open-side up in a deep saucepan, cover with boiling water, bring to the boil and boil for 10 minutes. Lift out with tongs and leave to drain upside down on a thick clean kitchen towel. Put on a baking tray lined with a few sheets of kitchen paper and keep warm in the oven set on its lowest setting until ready to fill with hot preserve. Alternatively, allow to cool completely before filling with cold preserve mixtures.

Sealing: as soon as the hot jam or chutney is in the jars, place a waxed paper circle directly on the top of the jam (these are available in packs of jam pot covers). Immediately seal tightly with a transparent jam pot cover and an elastic band or use a screw-top lid. Avoid covering preserves that have started to cool as this will shorten their storage life and encourage mould to form. For chutneys and preserves with vinegar, make sure the seals used are non-corrosive. Half-filled jars of any type of preserve should be cooled, covered and kept in the fridge, then used within a month.

REDUCED-SUGAR **PLUM JAM**

Victoria plums are the classic fruit for making jam and they have a good setting quality. This recipe uses less sugar than usual methods, but still gives a good set and delicious sharp flavour. Use the same method and quantities for similar stoned fruit, and also for berry fruits, though the set will be softer.

PREPARATION
10 minutes + cooling

COOKING TIME
4¾ hours on High

MAKES
About 1 kg (2 lb 3 oz)

1 kg (2 lb 3 oz) ripe Victoria plums, washed
500 g (1 lb 2 oz) jam sugar with pectin

1 Halve the plums and remove the stones, then roughly chop up the flesh. Put in the slow cooker and stir in the sugar.

2 Switch the slow cooker on to High, and cook, uncovered, stirring occasionally, for about 15 minutes, until the sugar has dissolved and formed a syrup. Cover with the lid and continue to cook for 2 hours, until very soft. Mash and stir the fruit after 1 hour to ensure even cooking.

3 Remove the lid and cook for a further 2 to 2½ hours, stirring occasionally, until thick and pulpy. To test for setting point, place a teaspoonful of jam on to a cold plate. Allow to cool, then push with your finger to see if the surface of the jam wrinkles. If it does, the jam is ready, if not, cook for a further 30 minutes and test again.

4 Carefully ladle the jam into warm, sterilized jam jars (see page 151). Cover the top with waxed paper discs and then seal with a transparent jam cover or screw-on lid while the jam is hot (see page 151). Allow to cool completely before storing for up to three months in a cool, dark place. Once opened, store in the fridge and use within a month.

COOK'S NOTE

The jam will become very hot during cooking, so make sure the cooker is positioned where it will stay undisturbed.

OLD-FASHIONED **LEMON CHEESE**

Homemade lemon cheese or curd is one of the finest of indulgencies, but it can be easily ruined by overcooking. The gentle slow cooker method makes the whole process worry-free and effortless.

PREPARATION
20 minutes + cooling

COOKING TIME
20 minutes on High
+ 1 hour on Low

MAKES
About 600 g (1 lb 5 oz)

3 unwaxed lemons
250 g (9 oz) caster sugar
125 g (4½ oz) unsalted butter
2 medium whole eggs
2 medium egg yolks

1 Measure the largest heatproof bowl that will fit inside your slow cooker dish with the lid on. Remove the bowl and put the slow cooker on High to preheat for 20 minutes while you prepare the curd.

2 Finely grate the lemons and put into the measured bowl, along with the sugar. Extract the lemon juice and strain through a sieve into the bowl. Cut the butter into small pieces and add to the bowl. Cover the bowl with a layer of foil, shiny-side down.

3 Stand the bowl in the slow cooker and pour in sufficient hot water to come halfway up the sides of the bowl. Cover with the lid and cook for 20 minutes until the butter has melted. Carefully remove the bowl from the cooker and stir the mixture until the sugar dissolves, then set aside to cool for 10 minutes. Reduce the setting to Low.

4 Beat the eggs and egg yolks, and strain through a sieve into the lemon mixture, whisking to combine. Re-cover the bowl with foil and return to the slow cooker. Cover with the lid and cook for about 1 hour, stirring halfway through, until thick enough to coat the back of a spoon.

5 Stir the mixture well, then carefully ladle the curd into warm, sterilized jam jars (see page 151). Cover the top with waxed paper discs and then seal with a transparent jam cover or screw-on lid while the cheese is hot (see page 151). Allow to cool completely before storing for up to two months in a very cool, dark place or the fridge. Once opened, store in the fridge and use within two weeks.

COOK'S NOTE

The foil layer below the lid helps retain a maximum amount of moisture when little liquid is used. Take care when removing the lid and foil, as the steam will be scalding.

FRUITY HOT **WINE TODDY**

Making a hot drink in your slow cooker will enable you to spend more time with your guests, and you can keep it warm until you're ready to serve it up.

PREPARATION
10 minutes

COOKING TIME
30 minutes on High
+ 40 minutes on Low

SERVES 6–8

50 g (2 oz) caster sugar
300 ml (½ pt) cranberry juice
6 cloves
1 small cinnamon stick, broken
¼ tsp ground nutmeg
1 bottle (75 cl) fruity red wine

2 eating apples
2 medium unwaxed oranges
150 g (5½ oz) seedless grapes
75 ml (2½ fl oz) orange-flavoured
    liqueur or brandy

1 Put the sugar in the slow cooker dish and add 150 ml (¼ pt) hot water. Stir until dissolved then pour in the cranberry juice. Switch the slow cooker on to High, add the spices and pour in the wine. Cover with the lid and cook for 30 minutes.

2 Meanwhile prepare the fruit. Wash the apples and remove the core. Slice thinly into rings. Wash the oranges and slice thinly. Wash and halve the grapes. Cover and set aside until required.

3 Add the fruit to the wine and stir in the liqueur or brandy. Cover, reduce the setting to Low, and heat through for a further 40 minutes. After this time, the wine is ready to serve but it can be kept hot for up to 4 hours by reducing the setting to Warm. Ladle the fruit and wine into heatproof glasses to serve.

COOK'S NOTE

For a lighter alternative, replace the cranberry juice with white grape juice, and use a medium-dry fruity white wine. Leave out the cloves.

USEFUL CONTACTS

STOCKISTS AND MANUFACTURERS

Amazon: www.amazon.com
Breville: www.breville.co.uk or www.breville.com (international)
Crockpot: www.crock-pot.com
Cuisinart: www.cuisinart.com
John Lewis: www.johnlewis.com
Lakeland Limited: www.lakeland.co.uk
Morphy Richards: www.morphyrichards.com
Robert Dyas: www.robertdyas.co.uk
Russell Hobbs: www.russell-hobbs.com
Tefal: www.tefal.co.uk or www.tefal.com (international)

BIBLIOGRAPHY

Atkinson Catherine, *The Slow Cooker Cookbook* (Lorenz Books, 2008)
FitzGibbon Theodora, *Crockery Pot Cooking* (Pan Books, 1978)
Grigson Sophie, *Sophie Grigson's Meat Course* (Network Books, 1995)
McGee Harold, *McGee on Food & Cooking* (Hodder & Stoughton, 2004)
Prestige Crock-Pot Slow Electric Cooker Cook Book
The Oxford Encyclopaedia of Food and Drink in America, Volume 2 (Oxford University Press, 2004)

ACKNOWLEDGEMENTS AND CREDITS

I would like to thank my mother, Margaret, for her help with the recipe testing, and friends Steve Brown and Kim MacKinnon for lending me their slow cookers to make my recipe testing a little easier. Thanks also to John Dakers and Alistair Brewster from Atholl Glens* for sourcing the mutton, and to Russell Hobbs for the beautiful slow cooker we used in the photography for the book. I would like to thank Sue Atkinson (and her assistants) for all the hard work and effort she put into making the food photography look so good. Finally, I would like to thank my editor Corinne – it's been a pleasure to work with you, and I wish you well for the future.

* Atholl Glens Organic Beef, Lamb and Mutton – a farming co-operative on the Atholl Estates in Highland Perthshire. Mail order delivery service available across the UK (www.athollglens.co.uk).

The publishers would like to thank Russell Hobbs for the loan of their slow cooker in the making of this book.

INDEX